T0327236

STUDYING FILMS

student editions

STUDYING CHUNGKING EXPRESS

Sean Redmond

Sean Redmond

is Senior Lecturer in Film Studies at Victoria University of Wellington, New Zealand. He has research interests in East Asian cinema, film authorship, genre, whiteness and stardom and celebrity. His latest book, the edited collection *The War Body on Screen*, was published by Continuum in 2008. He is the author of *Studying Blade Runner* for Auteur.

Acknowledgements

Thanks to Craig Skinner and to all my students on the Black and Asian Cinema Elective at Southampton Institute and Victoria University of Wellington.

Dedication

to Erin Rose - made of Stardust.

First published in 2004; revised 'student edition' first published in 2008 by Auteur, The Old Surgery, 9 Pulford Road, Leighton Buzzard LU7 1AB
www.auteur.co.uk
Copyright © Auteur 2008

Series design: Nikki Hamlett
Cover image © BFI Stills
All stills © BFI except pages 37, 69, 74, 76 and 78, taken from the Region 2 DVD of *Chungking Express*, distributed by Artificial Eye
Set by AMP Ltd, Dunstable, Bedfordshire
Printed and bound in Poland; produced by Polskabook

British Library Cataloguing-in-Publication Data
A catalogue record for this book is available from the British Library

ISBN 978-1-903663-80-6

Contents

Factsheet

Chungking Express (Chong ging sen lin) 1994, Hong Kong
Running Time   104 min
Certificate   15
Production Companies   Jet Tone Production Co.

Key credits

Director: Wong Kar-wai
Screenplay: Wong Kar-wai
Producer: Chan Ye-Cheng
Executive Producer: Chan Pui-wah
Production Designer: William Chang
Director of Photography: Chris Doyle
Editors: William Chang, Kai Kit-wai, Kwong Chi-leung
Music: Frankie Chan and Roel A. Garcia
Visual Effects: Cheng Xiaolong

Cast

Woman in Blonde Wig: Brigitte Lin
Cop 663:   Tony Leung
Faye: Faye Wong
Cop 223:   Takeshi Kaneshiro
Air Hostess: Valerie Chow
Manager of Midnight Express: Chen Jinquan

Synopsis

Chungking Express is split into two loosely connecting love stories. In the first, Cop 223, a regular at the Midnight Express takeaway, has been jilted by his long-time girlfriend. Melancholic and lonely, he counts down a date for their possible reunion, using the purchase and consumption of date stamped cans of pineapple – his girlfriend's favourite food – to do this. One night, on his birthday, having given up all hope of such a reunion, he finds himself drinking alone in a seedy bar. It is here that he promises to fall in love with the very next woman to walk in. A mysterious 'blonde' appears, and the two of them eventually spend a platonic night together in a hotel. In a corresponding sub-plot, the Blonde Woman has also been marked out as someone who is concerned with time passing: she has been threatened with execution for letting a drug deal go sour. After spending the night with Cop 223, she kills her drugs boss and makes good her escape, leaving a recorded 'happy birthday' message for Cop 223 on his pager.

In the second love story, two parallels with the first emerge: Cop 663 has also been dumped by his girlfriend, an air hostess, and he is also a regular at the Midnight Express takeaway. Cop 663 mourns the loss of his girlfriend through 'remembering' rituals in his/their flat. He invests objects with feelings and emotions such as his towel that he accuses of weeping. Faye, who works at the Midnight Express, begins to obsess over him, using the key left by his former girlfriend at the takeaway, to sneak into his apartment. She fills it with objects of her own such as clothes, canned food, goldfish and new towels, creating a 'home' with Cop 663 even though they have never really had a conversation. Cop 663 eventually catches her there but she runs away. Later on, at the Midnight Express, they make a date, but she fails to turn up, having decided in the meantime that she is going to be an air hostess, a position that will allow her to escape to her fantasy destination, California. After a year has passed, she returns to the Midnight Express to learn that Cop 663 has also changed his identity – he is settling in as its new owner. The film ends with the unresolved enigma that they may (or may not) fly off to California together.

Introduction: The Sensuous Intimacy of *Chungking Express*

'Knowing someone doesn't mean keeping them.
People change. A person may like pineapple today and
something else tomorrow.' Blonde Woman (Brigitte Lin)

Chungking Express is a startling film: its intoxicating
imagery and 'pop' inflected sound banks bombard the senses
from the very first moment of the film, and its dislocated
narrative and fragmentary plotting invite the audience to
question and to puzzle their way through it's entire length.
The key protagonists seem to float in and out of the action
like spectres or ghosts, unable or unwilling to communicate
or commit in concrete gestures and signs, preferring instead
to 'talk' through the device of the confessional voice-over
monologue, delivered only when all the other characters
cannot hear their sad or enigmatic refrains.

Jump-cuts, elliptical and 'stretch printing' editing techniques confuse the relationship between time and space and symbolically problematise character relationships, so that, for example, at one moment, in one shot, the foreground of an event can happen in slow-motion while the background can happen in quick time, blurring horizontal and vertical planes of action, isolating the character(s) because of the way they seem to co-exist in two different and yet simultaneous realities. Garish colours, bright and dull electric lights, and neon advertising screens dominate the mise-en-scène so that scene after scene appears pregnant with visual metaphors, not least the expressionistic signifiers of loss and regret, such as clocks ticking ever onwards, outside of human control. Commerce, food, speeding/congested traffic and crowds of people endlessly caught in movement, fill the screen to bursting, pointing to what seems, at first, to be a lack of intimacy in a postmodern world speeded up to an inhuman rhythm and tempo. But which, with a more detailed look, arguably represents a new form of sensuous intimacy, an intimacy that the film champions.

A *sensuous intimacy* fuelled by glossy globalisation, constant media communication and heterogeneous population flows, all of which open up the film's inhabitants to new and enriching (or at least transformative) experiences in consumption, movement, cultural proximity and existential impermancy. Marc Siegal has suggested that each of Wong's films can be read as 'indices of a public world of new intimacies' (2001: 280), where people learn to live and love together *through* letting the intoxication of speed, electrified imagery and consumer goods get into their veins and arteries.

This, then, is the aching beauty of *Chungking Express*, one where isolated characters bare their souls to people they hardly know, in cities constantly on the move, constantly charged, as time rushes by without a pause button in sight. This is the film that Quentin Tarantino confessed had made him cry because 'I am just so happy to love a movie this much', and this is the film which 'introduced' Wong Kar-wai to western audiences and to widespread critical claim. While *Chungking Express* appears high concept, politically lightweight and saturated in the codes and conventions of the MTV pop music video or the 'bubble-gum' action flick, its interior is actually laced with the most profound commentary on contemporary life. The film is as sophisticated, complicated and as artistically compelling as any contemporary experimental art film or social realist text. The beauty in the film is also there precisely because it is Wong Kar-wai directing: he is the perfect example of an auteur or visionary film-maker, and *Chungking Express* is perhaps one of the best examples of his filmwork.

This study of *Chungking Express* is an attempt to understand the complexity at the heart of this challenging film – to get close to its elegant and yet troubling beauty, and to make sense of its recurring motifs, metaphors, and contemplations on the human condition. Through textual, contextual and historical analysis, the majesty, melancholy and intimacy of the film emerges, as does its rightful place as one of the most important films made *anywhere in the world*, in the last fifteen years. The guide is a journey into the sensuous intimacy of *Chungking Express*, where tins of pineapple come to stand for yearning, desire, and the profound repercussions that a change in personal taste can have on who you are, who you can be with, and what you can (ever) become.

Through *Studying Chungking Express* one is introduced to a number of core theories and recurring themes that circulate in film studies and which are addressed at examination level. *Chungking Express*, then, can be used as a vehicle to get students interested in and familiar with 'foreign language' films, Art Cinema, questions of film authorship, mise-en-scène analysis, representation and identity, and independent film production. At the time of writing this guide *Chungking Express* is a cited text in the A Level Film Studies syllabus, and is regularly used as an introductory text to film analysis at undergraduate level. Once one 'opens up' *Chungking Express* to serious critical and contextual analysis one finds a treasure trove of salient issues that feed right back into the heart of what drives Film Studies more generally. Enjoy. *Eat.*

1. Wider Contexts

While the close textual analysis of a film is at the cornerstone of a great deal of work undertaken by film academics and critics, placing a film in terms of its wider contexts, looking outwards, so to speak, to its production history, reception and to the culture that it emerges from, is also centrally important. One reads a film not just through its formal, aesthetic qualities but through the concepts of ideology, representation, identity and power, and to do this one has go *outside the text* – to the politics of the age – to then bring text and context together in mutually supportive structures of meaning. One can argue that one cannot fully understand *Chungking Express* without reference to the Art film, film movements and the Hong Kong New Wave cinema from which it emerged; the political issues around national sovereignty, independence and governorship that were dominating social and political life in Hong Kong at the time the film was made; and the biography and film-making practices of the film's director/auteur, Wong Kar-wai. All of these 'wider contexts' will be now be explored in turn.

Film Movements, the Hong Kong New Wave and Art Cinema

When one reflects upon the great formal upheavals in the history of film and cinema, one is immediately presented with the concept of the film movement. The revolutions in the language and aesthetics of film that accompanied the emergence of Soviet Formalism, German Expressionism, the French New Wave and, more recently, Dogme 95, were driven by the cohesive and cohering energies of what were sometimes only ever a loosely formed group of film-makers who wanted – although not always consciously – to do something ground-breaking, something challenging, something inherently revolutionary with the medium of film.

Film movements are nearly always cohering forces of change and transformation, with their film-makers radically reshaping the way narratives can be told and interpreted not only short term but long term, leaving their mark on the trajectory of cinema long after the movement has ended or been usurped by another. One can argue that a film movement can be defined by the following five interconnecting elements or components.

First, film movements are often at the forefront of innovation and experimentation, and this 'avant garde' instinct can itself be seen to manifest in different ways. For example, innovation in and experimentation with technology can often free up film-makers to create new visual and narrative canvasses – canvasses that allow them to play with light, framing, focus, depth, and shot composition and order. In terms of the French New Wave (1959–1963) Raymond Durgnat suggests:

The invention of fast emulsions led to low budgets, minimum crews, location work and 'independent' finance. These new styles in aesthetics and production accompany new thematic perspectives. (in Cook, 1999: 81)

Jean-Luc Godard's *A bout de souffle (Breathless)* (1959) is the archetypal French New Wave film: made on a tiny budget of 400,000 French francs, the film was shot and edited (by Godard, his first feature) in just over a month. Its homage to and subversion of the American gangster and film noir picture is manufactured out of an editing technique that disrupts spatial and temporal relations. Godard perfected the jump-cut and elliptical edit to crack open the coherency and verisimilitude of the fictional film world, rendering the narrative a fractured experience, and the characters abstracted enigmas. *A bout de souffle* uses its mobile cameras, natural locations and the city mise-en-scène to reflect upon and critique the American culture and American film that had come to so dominate the popular media post-war. As we shall shortly see, there are strong echoes here of the way *Chungking Express* is structured and to the homage motifs and metaphors found in its 'new wave' anti-realist interior.

One can transform film-making practices then, in what might be called *relational contexts*, where technological innovation works its alchemy on/in film language and representation, and where they simultaneously work their way into technological innovation, producing systematic challenges to the way films had been made before, to the way films had been hitherto structured and narrated, and to the images, values and ideologies that are often seen, by those who 'author' film movements, to emotionally cripple conventional or mainstream film-making at the time.

Second, and in a related point, film movements often challenge, oppose and eventually usurp existing, dominant film-making practices. One only has to return to the example of the French New Wave and François Truffaut's savage critique of the 'quality' French cinema that came to prominence in the 1940s, and which he argued stifled film expression in France because of their fondness for empty literary scripts and heritage inspired settings. As Annette Kuhn observes, the French New Wave's:

> **Apparent improvisations in camera technique (the long take, the freeze frame), editing (the jump cut), dialogue, plot and performance were all deployed because cinema was seen for the first time not as a neutral form through which something else (literature or 'reality') could be transmitted, but as a specific aesthetic system, a**

language in itself. (in Cook, 1999: 80)

Third, film movements are often driven by enigmatic and passionate individuals (friends, comrades) who share a common philosophy on film-making, and a similar (radical) political agenda. The Marxist, socialist ideologies of those working in Soviet Formalism in the 1920s and post-war Italian neo-realism, are two such instances, employing film to capture, in different ways, the traumas and pressures of ordinary working-class life. However, there is no better recent example of a political manifesto being welded to film practice than Dogme 95's Vow of Chastity, which is re-printed in full opposite.

For the Dogme 95 film-makers, the film text can get close to some sort of social and political truth but to do so must avoid all the artificial techniques employed by much of mainstream cinema. The Dogme quest is for an authentic cinema in an entertainment landscape made up of artifice. Their Vow of Chastity implies that the least amount of technological intervention in the film-making process makes for a more honest, realistic aesthetic. One can contextualise this vow in terms of the predominance of special effects, glossy visuals, fast cutting and anthemic soundtracks that had come to dominate a great deal of World Cinema at the time that this pledge was written – including much of the hi-octane film work of the Hong Kong New Wave (including *Chungking Express*).

Fourth, film movements are often initially nation specific, emerging out of or because of fault lines and inadequacies in the national cinema of the time. The industry is often felt to be moribund, conservative and bureaucratic, and a wave of what are considered to be radical, often young film-makers emerge to chastise, challenge and ultimately overthrow the status

'The Vow of Chastity'

I swear to submit to the following set of rules drawn up and confirmed by DOGME 95:

1. Shooting must be done on location. Props and sets must not be brought in. (If a particular prop is necessary for the story, a location must be chosen where this prop is to be found.)

2. The sound must never be produced apart from the images or vice versa. (Music must not be used unless it occurs where the scene is being shot.)

3. The camera must be hand-held. Any movement or immobility attainable in the hand is permitted. (The film must not take place where the camera is standing; shooting must take place where the film takes place.)

4. The film must be in colour. Special lighting is not acceptable. (If there is too little light for exposure the scene must be cut or a single lamp be attached to the camera.)

5. Optical work and filters are forbidden.

6. The film must not contain superficial action. (Murders, weapons, etc. must not occur.)

7. Temporal and geographical alienation are forbidden. (That is to say that the film takes place here and now.)

8. Genre movies are not acceptable.

9. The film format must be Academy 35mm.

10. The director must not be credited.

Furthermore I swear as a director to refrain from personal taste! I am no longer an artist. I swear to refrain from creating a 'work', as I regard the instant as more important than the whole. My supreme goal is to force the truth out of my characters and settings. I swear to do so by all the means available and at the cost of any good taste and any aesthetic considerations.

Thus I make my VOW OF CHASTITY

Copenhagen, Monday 13 March 1995

On behalf of DOGME 95, Lars von Trier, Thomas Vinterberg

quo. Such film movements may be politically motivated, such as the black workshop movement (Sankofa) that emerged in Britain in the 1980s. This movement attempted to make radical and thought-provoking films for black audiences who were denied access to their own representations because of the white hegemony that shaped independent and commercial film-making in Britain at the time. The quasi-documentary *Handsworth Songs* explored the 1984 race riots but from a black point of view and through experimental narrative and editing techniques.

Nonetheless, finally, film movements very quickly come to shape and affect film-makers and film-making practices across national borders, and for a longer period of time than the historical juncture in which they emerge. Soviet Formalism, German Expressionism, the French New Wave, Italian Neo-realism and, in terms of the contemporary film landscape, the Hong Kong New Wave, come to witness the reach of their interventions and influences on a global and trans-historical stage.

The Hong Kong New Wave

> **The (new wave) films articulate a Hong Kong identity that is connected with and detached from both the Western world and the Chinese world, and they often refute the official 'success' story while attempting to construct a native memory. (Yau, 2001: 5)**

Hong Kong cinema has arguably gone through two 'new waves' of innovation and experimentation in the last 25 years, although each wave overlaps in terms of personnel, film form, the play with genre and the concern for expressing local issues and problems. The 'first' Hong Kong New Wave emerged in the late 1970s/early 1980s, ushered in by the films of Tsui Hark, Ann Hui, John Woo, Ringo Lam and Patrick Tam. The emergence can be seen in the context of a developing film culture in Hong Kong, with the Hong Kong International Film Festival, launched in 1977, crystallising this newfound confidence and interest in cine literacy. Many of the New Wave directors attended colleges in North America or England (Bordwell, 2000: 69) and developed their skills in television production before going on to direct full-length features. This 'apprenticeship' allowed them access to global references in art, film and popular culture, and enabled them to bring higher production values to the film-making process.

New Wave films can also be considered in terms of the revival of Cantonese Cinema, and with it the local audience's interest in going to the cinema. Not only did these New Wave film-makers make experimental, commercial films but also they adopted the 'language' of their 'native' citizens, Cantonese, and they filled their films with political issues that emanated from the local context. As Bordwell (2000: 69) notes:

> **Unlike earlier generations, they took Hong Kong, not traditional China, as their subject, and many tackled contemporary social and psychological problems. Some made edgy, mildly, experimental works, perhaps best exemplified by Ann Hui's *The Secret* (1979) and Tsui Hark's *Dangerous Encounter – First Kind* (1980).**

Tsui Hark's work is perhaps seminal here: one finds the conscious play with and subversion of traditional Chinese genres such as the martial arts film and the swordplay fantasy; one discovers a radical experimentation with film form, where camera movement, framing, speed of cutting and special effects conjure up the most breathtaking, kinetic, intoxicating planes of action; and one finds, at least in an allegorical sense, a concern with the loss of tradition and the sense of a foreboding crisis hanging over the inhabitants of Hong Kong Island.

The 'second' New Wave emerged in the early 1990s and it is here that the work of Wong Kar-wai appeared as the pivotal force in transcoding film form and opening up Hong Kong cinema to the critical claim afforded to much of European Art Cinema and 'independent' cinema in general. Hong Kong cinema went through a creative and commercial slump in the early 1990s. A repetitive cycle of poorly produced formula films emerged, and in turn ticket sales fell. This local demise was compounded by a decline in the overseas market for Hong Kong films which normally accounted 'for between 30 and 80% of the total income of each production' (Kwai-Cheung Lo, 2001: 265). On top of this, half a million of the island's most talented artists had left, principally because of the spectre of the hand-over to China in 1997. This left a chasm in terms of new blood coming through to make innovative films.

In this cultural vacuum, however, a new breed of film-maker eventually emerged who wanted to invest their creative energies in transforming the form and content of Hong Kong cinema. They attempted to re-interpret the concept of the local in a postmodern world where, it was felt, almost all barriers to communication, travel and consumption had been eroded. Kwai-Cheung Lo suggests that:

For new wave directors ... like Allen Fong, Ann Hui, Stanley Kwan ... localism no longer pertains to the culture and customs of a particular place. It is thought of in relation to other cultures and other localities, rather than simply being a thing that stresses its selfsame identity. (2001: 264)

The second Hong Kong New Wave, then, seems to be particularly informed/transformed by 'borderless capitalisation', the spectre of Mainland China, Western, particularly American, culture, and by the traditions of (European) Art Cinema. In this heady mix of cultural and political change and uncertainty, the *oeuvre* of Wong Kar-wai appeared, bringing with his work the worries over China, Americanisation, postmodern isolation and identity crisis, and the aesthetics and politics of the Art Cinema tradition.

Wong Kar-wai's experimentalism in narrative form and editing techniques are in fact argued to be closer to the work of Jean-Luc Godard and/or Alain Renais, and because he uses the materials of popular culture in his films, he is seen to be a commentator on Hong Kong's postmodern condition rather than just a passive receptor of/for it. In short, one can argue that Wong Kar-wai's filmwork bears all the hallmarks of the (European) Art Cinema tradition.

Art Cinema

Art Cinema is usually defined by its difference and opposition to the mainstream, and particularly to the Hollywood mainstream that is seen to threaten other national cinemas not only in terms of market share but also in terms of its totalising 'classical' film form. David Bordwell suggests that, 'Art Cinema defines itself explicitly against the classical narrative mode, and especially against the cause–effect linkage of events' (2002: 95), while Steve Neale contends that, 'art is thus the space in which an indigenous cinema can develop and make its critical and economic mark' (2002: 104). Drawing on Bordwell and Neale's work, the characteristics or qualities of Art Cinema can be defined as follows.

Art Cinema tends to have a loose narrative structure: not a structure, then, that is based on a cause-and-effect or linear logic, as is much the case in mainstream cinema, but one that can be dislocated, multi-strand and opaque. Such narratives allow fully rounded characters to emerge, who as a consequence can explore their traumas, fantasises and desires in cinematic spaces designed to allow them to narrate such psychological states. These highly charged and complex characters experience social, emotional and psychosexual problems and it is the function of Art Cinema to explore these. This is at the expense of dramatic narrative action and the 'logical' movement to resolution and closure where all loose ends are tied up and social order is restored. In Art Cinema, narrative progression is as much about the search for abstract truths, and closure is often more about aperture, and unresolved or unsolvable enigmas. As Bordwell writes:

> **The Art Cinema is less concerned with action than reaction; it is a cinema of psychological effects in search of their causes. The dissection of feeling is often represented explicitly as therapy and cure, but even when it is not, the forward flow of causation is braked and characters pause to seek the aetiology of their feelings. (2000: 96)**

In the harrowing Belgian film *Funny Games* (Haneke, 1997) two young strangers walk into the home of a well-off family and spend the entire film torturing them. The audience is not given any character information except the very spare details that emerge on screen. There are no sub-plots, no dramatic action in the Hollywood sense, and there are no heroes and villains structured in binary opposition. Good does not triumph over evil and any exploration of morality is blurred because of the lack of signposts or variables given in the film. All there is, in fact, is the *will to power* that emerges between the central protagonists, shot in claustrophobic lengths and angles so that one just anticipates that escape is impossible. At one point in the film the narrative as such stops as one of the male bullies reaches for a television remote control and seeks to literally rewind the film to a point where he is again in control of the events. This self-conscious act, where the audience watch the film rewind and then play out to a different outcome, opens the text to a greater range of meanings and possible interpretations. The film ends as it begins, with the two young strangers walking into another home, we can only guess, to start the cycle all over again. The film, then, displays all the hallmarks of the Art film, and some of its sparse and self-conscious techniques can also be found in *Chungking Express*.

Art Cinema is not a 'blockbuster' or genre driven cinema but a cinema of visual beauty, thought-provoking contemplation and of experimentation in film form. Art Cinema rejects the artifice and the consumerism of the Hollywood or popular cinema machine, for authenticity and epiphany moments, whether this is played out through social realist codes or anti-realist devices. According to Bordwell:

> **A conception of realism also affects the film's spatial and temporal construction, but the Art Cinema's realism here encompasses a spectrum of possibilities. The options range from a documentary factuality to intense psychological subjectivity (when the two impulses meet in the same film, the familiar 'illusion/reality' dichotomy of the art cinema results). (2000: 97)**

Art cinema is also the location for the Deleuzean Time Image in which characters find themselves in situations where they are unable to act and react in a direct, immediate way, leading to what he calls is a breakdown in the sensor-motor system. The image set free from its temporal and spatial coordinates becomes 'a pure optical and aural image', and one that 'comes into relation with a virtual image, a mental or mirror image' (Deleuze, 1995: 52). In a Time Image Art Film, 'sheets of past [can] coexist in a non-chronological order' (1989: xii), and characters as a consequence are forced inside themselves to find answers to their temporal dislocation. The inner journey becomes a privileged narrative form in Art Cinema, with characters in a more passive role, and themes centered on inner mental imagery, irrationality and emotional and psychic breakdown.

The Time Image shocks the spectator out of their engagement with the narrative: rational or concrete temporal links between shots – the cornerstone of mainstream cinema – give way to 'incommensurable', non-rational links. Because of these non-rational links between shots, vacant and disconnected spaces begin to appear. Deleuze calls these 'any-space-whatevers' (ibid.). The spectator, when faced with such an empty or dislocated space, is forced out of the fiction of the film and into their own memories. Deleuze called 'time' the highest pursuit of cinema, and Art Cinema is its greatest proponent.

The ambiguity and complexity of Art Cinema requires a unifying artistic voice, an auteur no less, who exists as a conscious presence in the film text, directing the audience's attention to their themes, obsessions and stylistics traits. The Art film 'foregrounds the author as a structure in the film's system' (ibid.). And in so doing draws attention to their authorship and to the film-making process itself. In fact, Art Cinema's mode of address assumes an educated, intelligent audience who can read the complex signs embedded in the film. This audience is imagined to be active, critical readers who possess the 'cultural capital' to read Art film texts at their deepest level.

Art Cinema, finally, is made solely for artistic or creative purposes, on a small scale, with small budgets, and the independent nature of the production gives more control over the film-making process to the director in question. This reinforces the strength of the argument that great art, by visionary directors, can emerge most successfully in the arena of Art Cinema.

When one tries to place Wong Kar-wai's *oeuvre* into this Art Cinema tradition one can immediately see a number of close affinities, especially in relation to *Chungking Express*. The film has a loose narrative structure with a high degree of internalised dramatic conflict shaping events. Nothing much happens in the film in terms of dramatic action, instead isolation: memory moments; and the passing of time provide the framework in which the story is told. *Chungking Express* has an opaque/open ending and a number of unresolved enigmas remain at the point of film's closure. We are not sure that Faye and Cop 663 will fly off to California together and because of the use of ellipses in the film, we are not sure why she has returned to Hong Kong. The central characters are angst ridden, lonely, haunted by the possibility that they have already missed their opportunities to fall in love. Masculinity and femininity seem to be in a state of crisis in the film, and so the usual 'mainstream' convention of having clearly differentiated roles for men and women collapse in the film. The Blonde Woman appears the most active, empowered, while Cop 223 spends most of the first love story moping, hording his ex-girlfriend's favourite food (just so that he can remain close to her). *Chungking Express* is marked by a great deal of visual beauty and the authorial signature of Wong Kar-wai can be found across the film both in terms of visual traits and recurring themes (such as the meaning of time). The film is highly subjective, experimental and yet mixes this with high levels of realism. The voice-over monologues delivered in the film create the impression that subjectivity is always marked by faulty memory. Editing techniques such as the jump-cut (where action is broken up) and stretch printing (where in one shot two different speeds of reality exist side-by-side) dislocate the action and blur the temporal relations in the film. *Chungking Express* was made using guerrilla-like methods of working – Wong Kar-wai shot the film very quickly, with a high degree of improvisation, and with crew he had used previously. In essence, he had complete control over the shoot and so this is clearly his Art film.

However, Wong Kar-wai's film work also bears the hallmark of a commercial film, as much influenced by Hollywood, advertising and MTV as it is by the Art Cinema tradition. *Chungking Express* is full of rapid cuts, glossy visuals and pop culture references. In fact, it is probably the synthesis of these sets of diverse influences that render the film so interesting, so artistically compelling. Marchetti makes sense of this hybridity by suggesting that:

> **...** *Chungking Express* **relies on Hollywood as a backdrop. It pastiches Hollywood genres like the policier, the gangster film, and the romantic comedy. It plays with a Hollywood/Hong Kong sense of stars and stardom, for example, Lin Quing-xia as Monroe; Faye Wong as Jean Seberg; Tony Leung somewhere between Cary Grant and a John Woo hero. It self-reflexively recognizes itself as a commodity for exchange within the international art film market. (2002: 306)**

In summary, one can argue that the fractured nature of *Chungking Express* stems from the political and social context that the film was made in, from Wong Kar-wai's own fractured upbringing and from his improvisational method of working. It is these 'facts' which will further confirm his credentials as a director with a truly unique cinematic vision.

Hong Kong Island and 1997

One can argue, with some justification, that there is nowhere on earth quite like Hong Kong. Six and half million people live there making it one of the most densely populated city-states in the world. The population is diverse and heterogeneous, made up of immigrants (mainly from China), ex-patriots (from the UK), transnational businessmen and 'workers', and travellers from all around the world. As a consequence the population of Hong Kong is always in flux, transient, with multiple cultures and national identities, sharing and communicating in the same 'always open' crowded spaces. Tradition exists alongside (post) modernity, and the culture(s) of the East sit at the same table as the cultures of the West, sometimes producing conflict and division. The concept of Diaspora is important here: not only are there many 'uprooted' people in Hong Kong but a constant state of metaphoric homelessness seems to define its citizens because of what seems to be a lack of a cohering centre.

Hong Kong never sleeps because it lives to produce (and transport) goods and services and to consume what has been produced and distributed. It is a city driven by commerce and capitalist freedoms. There are no limits on the numbers of hours that people can work. Hong Kong has the world's largest container port; is the top exporter of toys, watches and candles; has the highest per capita consumption of brandy and Rolls-Royse; and remains the regional centre for banking, shipping, ship building, cargo services and insurances. (Stokes and Hoover, 1999)

At the same time, Hong Kong is a city plagued by over-crowding and homelessness (property prices are terrifically high and many people live in small, crowded apartments – space is at a premium); there is high and low level corruption; drug trafficking; contraband; high rates of organised crime; and a higher than average suicide rate amongst the young. In short, Hong Kong is a two-headed beast: one head offers the citizen the promise (reality) of wealth and satisfying consumption; the other head offers misery, squalour and violence. This economic schizophrenia is compounded by Hong Kong's history and its uncertain present projected as some sort of future apocalypse because of the pending, total transfer of power to the Chinese. Janice Tong captures what she calls this 'horizon of loss' in prosaic terms:

> Hong Kong in the mid-1990s was experiencing the state of its own disappearance. A shroud of uncertainty has bathed the city-state since the 1984 Sino-British Joint Declaration returning Honk Kong to China. But even before this, the history of Hong Kong has always reflected a city in flux: from its origin as a territory of the Qing Dynasty, Hong Kong was then annexed to the British for a period of 99 years after the Opium War, during which time it also experienced a period of Japanese occupation. In its status as a British colonial-state it thrived as an entrepot, an unparalleled 'nexus' through which the cultural and economic traffic of the East and West passed and still passes. (2003: 48)

Hong Kong might also be termed a postmodern city *on the edge of time*: people are perceived to be always on the move, rushing about, on their way to work, to eat, to buy, to sell, in a city where so much on offer is the equivalent of the world's fastest fast-food. This constant movement interrupts and problematises social interaction and the possibility of stable relationships so that for many Hong Kong is experienced as a lonely city. Trying to exist in a city where everyone and everything is on the move (including 'language') causes people to lose the sense of who they are, what they are and where they are in the city. Hong Kong is an unstable space and the people are unstable within it. In one sense, time and space are 'uncoupled' because travel, movement and interaction happen in the mediated universe of television screens, radio jingles, neon advertising, and (Western) branded goods and services. Hong Kong's spatial fluidity produces the sense that reality there is itself transient and on the move, more hyperreal than real, more ephemeral than concrete. In this city of aching dreams, people suffer an eternal identity crisis, very much like the city itself – caught between East and West, Cantonese and Mandarin, tradition and modernity, independence and governorship, wealth and poverty, nothing sits easily in/on Hong Kong. This city of aching beauty, Hong Kong, with its mix of people, its unresolved history, its break-neck trajectory, its commodification, its teeming spatial organisation and its 'collective' identity crisis is central to the way *Chungking Express* can be read and understood.

At the core of the film is this heterogeneous city itself, with all the central characters looking, longing for love, for intimacy, in a city too fast to get a hold of. At the core of the film are the metaphors of time, loss and crisis that speak to the impending hand-over to China in 1997, and to the postmodern condition where so much that matters slips outside the control or reach of one's liquid hands. At the core of the film is an engagement with popular (American) culture, commodity capitalism, and the desire to be whole, complete, in a city of fracture and existential dislocation. At the core of the film, arguably, is a warm embrace of all this shock of the new, an embrace made up from a love of pop art and kitsch culture, of fast-food and fast people. In short, at the core of *Chungking Express* is an ambivalent, perhaps contradictory exploration of Hong Kong at the time the film was made. In fact, Janice Tong suggests that:

> **Wong's image-narrative in *Chungking Express* presents Hong Kong as a city with an absent centre. In its place, we find a mobile state of rupture where images, space, time, characters and narratives fold in upon each other, weaving a skein of images that threaten to slip from our gaze. (2003: 54)**

Chungking Express is largely set in two contrasting locations: Chungking Mansion in Tsimshatsui, and Central, consisting of Lan Kwai Fong, where the Midnight Express can be found, and the Mid-level escalators. Chungking Mansion is a haven for tourists and backpackers looking for cheap accommodation, and also has a reputation as a seedy district with some drug and prostitution problems. Originally, Tsimshatsui was the Indian quarter renowned for its food and textiles and its cosmopolitan, multi-cultural sentiments remain. By contrast, both Lan Kwai Fong and the Mid-level escalator areas are home to Western bars and expensive restaurants – 'yuppie' districts – and they attract people on the move, people who want to consume. Wong himself has suggested that both these places function as 'microcosms of Hong Kong' (quoted in Lalanne et al., 1997) and it is the sense that these local/global, busy/empty, risky/sterile districts allow the themes of the film to unfold in richly metaphoric environments. They are also areas 'personal' to Wong Kar-wai.

Wong Kar-wai: A Fractured Biography

Wong Kar-wai was born in Shangai in 1958, but moved to the Tsimsha Tsui area of Hong Kong at the age of five because of his father's occupation (Sailor). His parents had intended the move to be temporary but because of the Chinese Revolution they remained there as exiles. Wong Kar-wai was a native Shanghainese speaker and so the move to Hong Kong required him to master the Cantonese dialect spoken there. As a child, he spent a great deal of time at the cinema with his mother, watching Mandarin films that he was familiar with and could understand. Wong's later filmic concerns with displacement, cultural differences and isolation arguably have their roots in his upbringing as an (exiled) immigrant, living in a run-down area of Hong Kong, itself an area full of fellow exiles, come-and-go tourists, and the global goods and services of monopoly capitalism sold legitimately and on the black market.

Wong's interest in creative art blossomed while he studied for a diploma in Graphic Design at Hong Kong Polytechnic. Here he became particularly interested in the photography of Robert Frank, Heni Cartier-Bresson and Richard Avedon. After he graduated in 1980, he enrolled in a TV drama training course organised by Hong Kong Television Broadcast (HKTB) and quickly became involved in writing scripts for serials and soap operas, most notably for the ratings winner *Don't Look Now*. Wong Kar-wai left HKTB in 1982 to become a full-time scriptwriter for feature films, working for Cinema City, one of the biggest commercial film-making studios in Hong Kong. Here he wrote up to a dozen scripts, including action, romance and romantic comedies. Wong considers that the best of these was for Patrick Tam's *Final Victory* (1996). It was during the writing of this that Wong Kar-wai conceived what would be his directorial debut, the gangster flick, *As Tears Go By* (1988).

Wong's early experiences in photography, film and television have arguably shaped his later filmwork. The Art Cinema aesthetics, which in part structure his films, clearly emerge from his love and experience of European art films and New Wave photography. His embrace of the popular and the commercial emerge from his own taste distinctions and the film-making traditions and methods of working that he found himself in when on the pay-role for HKTB and Cinema City. His 'authorial' desire to control all the elements of a film, from pre-production to post-production, stems from an experience in both film and television where commerce and ratings (producers) called the shots and art, as a consequence, played second fiddle.

Wong Kar-wai is largely an improvisational director. He scripts sequences the night before they are filmed; he doesn't hold rehearsals prior to or *during* shooting and regularly re-works scripts during shooting, only giving the actors their provisional dialogue after he has arrived on set for that day's filming. Wong Kar-wai demands an awful lot from his actors, subjecting them to a large number of retakes so that he ends up with numerous options when it comes to cutting the film, and because it also produces noteworthy performances. Marc Siegal summarises Wong Kar-wai's perspective:

> **This strategy is a necessary one given the context of film-making in Hong Kong, where films are produced at such a quick rate and actors, who are making a number of films at the same time, are not able to 'enter the world' of the particular film Wong is shooting ... By exhausting his performers, Wong is able to extract from them performances of great intensity and intimacy. (2001: 288-289)**

In the course of a Wong Kar-wai film, whole plots, narrative outcomes, reams of dialogue, a character's motivations or actual role in a film can change and even disappear, not least because reels and reels of footage are left on the cutting room floor. For example, none of the two weeks of footage taken in Brigitte Lin's home made in into *Chungking Express*. Christopher Doyle, Wong Kar-wai's 'resident' director of photography has said that a Wong Kar-wai film is like a fat man's feet. They get him where he wants to go, sometimes slowly, but he can't ever see them until he sits down at the end of the day. The analogy suggests that Wong Kar-wai never really knows where his films will end up until he gets them into the editing room.

Wong Kar-wai controls almost every aspect of a film's production and in so doing attracts the moniker of auteur or visionary film-maker. As Martinez suggests:

> **Since 1988 when he made ... *As Tears Goes By*, he has scripted all his films, and controlled all other aspects on the auteur model. He explores a universe of personal themes and obsessions, selects the actors, locations and duration of the shoot (often changed to allow for improvisation), takes sole charge of the final cut and, of course, the background music and songs, selecting the composer (generally Danny Chung or Frankie Chan) and the songs or extracts that he wants to us. (1997: 29)**

Chungking Express is Wong Kar-wai's third film, made over a two-month period because of a break in filming his big budget *Ashes of Time*. Wong Kar-wai wrote most of the scenes for *Chungking Express* in a Holiday Inn coffee shop, bringing together 'script ideas he had been considering for years' (Bordwell, 2000: 283). He shot the film in conception or sequence order, whenever and wherever there was enough light. By all accounts the film was highly improvised and extended Wong Kar-wai's use of experimental editing techniques and foregrounded his formal appetite for loosely connected narratives.

In many respects, then, there is a close affinity with Godard's *A bout de souffle*. *Chungking Express* was also made 'on the run', from the pressures of *Ashes of Time*, with little shooting time available, on a small budget, with little written down in the way of script or dialogue, and with 'Hollywood as a backdrop' (Marchetti, 2000: 306). What emerges is a radical film that self-consciously announces (proclaims) its radicalism to World Cinema, while saying something profound about the human condition in a postmodern Hong Kong desperate for definition. *Chungking Express*: an Art-Pop film, emerging out of the Hong Kong New Wave, with a contemplative auteur at the helm. Cinema will never be the same again.

2. Narrative Analysis

Two Stories Out of Time

> The two stories are quite independent. What puts them together is that they are both love stories. I think a lot of city people have a lot of emotions but sometimes they can't find the people to express them to. (Wong Kar-wai, quoted in Bordwell, 2000: 283)

Chungking Express has a split structure with two 'separate' love stories being told largely in succession and chronological order. These stories of 'loss' and longing overlap and connect, nonetheless, because of the way key events, overriding desires and dreams double up, parallel and echo each other in the film. In *Chungking Express* the central narrative moments are stitched together in abstract and metaphorical cycles rather than through a strictly linear structure where cause-and-effect can be read through particular actions. In fact, chance encounters and approximate notions of intimacy energise the plot rather than some adherence to goal or action orientated events. David Bordwell defines the plot of *Chungking Express* as one that 'is built out of a daunting number of minutely varied repetitions of locales and routines. As these cycles compare characters and situations, cause and effect become less important than parallels among congruent or contrasting aspects of love'. (2000: 283)

This sense of a constantly reoccurring 'déjà vu' between people, places and intimacies emerges from the start of the film. At the beginning of *Chungking Express*, while Cop 223 is chasing a criminal down a crowded corridor, he drifts past what will become his love interest in the story – the 'Blonde Woman' – announcing in voice-over that, 'at our closest point, we were just 0.01cm apart from each other. Fifty-five hours later, I was in love with this woman'. At the end of the first 'love' story, after Cop 223 has received the Blonde Woman's paged birthday message, he retreats to the Midnight Express where he bumps into Faye and launches the next love story, with the voice-over, 'six hours later she fell in love with another man'. All four of the main characters appear briefly in the first love story of the film, providing poetic instances and connections of lovers looking, longing, desperate for the chance encounter that will, might or possibly could change their destinies forever – as one quickly comes to realise, the future is decidedly shaky in *Chungking Express*.

The 'other man', Cop 663, is introduced in the film ordering fish and chips for his air hostess girlfriend – a change from the chef's salad that he would usually order for her. Not only does the reference to chef's salad echo Cop 223's eating of four chef's salads the night he is 'romancing' the Blonde Woman while she sleeps, but it also heralds the breakdown of 663's relationship with his air hostess girlfriend. Both 'girlfriends' in the second love story eventually share the same profession, while the Blonde Woman loses her drug couriers at the airport (with *flight* possibly now being her only escape, especially once she commits to killing the drug lord).

Water, tears and rain are recurring symbols in both love stories. Cop 223 goes running to get over his broken heart, because 'running evaporates bodily fluid so there's none left for tears'. The Blonde Woman wears a raincoat because she thinks 'it will rain', summing up her own melancholic cry as she walks alone (lonely) in the brooding Hong Kong cityscape. In the second love story, Cop 663 accuses his towel of weeping, and when the flat is flooded he thinks that he has been caught in a tidal wave of remorse and melancholy. In fact, in terms of the relay of tears in and between both stories, one can argue that the tears that Cop 223 sweats out of his body in the first love story become the origins of the flood in the second love story. The 'flood' relay between both stories is extended to other similarities: both cops struggle to sleep; both cops spend a platonic first night/day with the Blonde Woman/Faye, each letting their muse sleep off their exhaustion in the hotel room/apartment; and both Faye and the Blonde Woman wear sunglasses, glasses that reflect objects caught in their vision.

Fast-food and convenience foods are also key recurring motifs in both stories, heavily connected to the themes of time passing and personal transformation. Cop 223 counts down the end of his affair with May through tins of pineapple dated 1 May – exactly 30 days from when she dumped him. The Blonde Woman is given a can of sardines with the date of 1 May on it, the deadline for the completion of her drug smuggling assignment. Cop 663 gives his girlfriend fish and chips for one night and this he reasons makes her realise that there are other 'options' available in life, including whom she can love. Faye replaces objects, including tins of sardines, at Cop 663's flat, and all of the central characters either meet or commit to meet in bars and restaurants (principally in the Midnight Express). Crucially, these are also the venues where they learn that love has somehow passed them by again, and again, and again.

The Midnight Express provides the anchoring point of contact in the film, enabling both love stories to cross paths. It is where both Cop 223 and Cop 663 go to eat, escape and find romance. It supplies the fast-food and the romantic interest for Cop 663, sparking character transformations and relationships. Faye secretly falls in love with Cop 663 in the short exchanges one has when serving/ordering food there. Cop 663's girlfriend leaves him because of the fish and chips prepared there; and Cop 663 gives up his job to run the joint just so he can touch/taste the food that brought him close to

Faye in the first place.

As Bordwell (2000) suggests, *Chungking Express* is full of images of mutability, such as clouds drifting, cigarette smoke rising, and its 'action' principally takes place in transient spaces, such as fast-food joints, bars, airports and hotel rooms. Through these images of drift and locations of movement, not a person or a 'thing' is able to stand still or root itself in a material present or a knowable tomorrow. In what are essentially metaphoric images and spaces for time itself, time is set to drift and to take on organic qualities that render it not only a force of transformation but also a force of loss and isolation simply because time cannot stop, not even for a second. The one device used to stop time – the freeze frame – is presented in past tense, shown only as a 'memory', when a character is looking backwards at a moment that couldn't be stopped or fully comprehended when it first happened.

The concept, the movement and the passing of time are central to the way the film's narrative works. In the first love story actual and symbolic time energises the plot and limits or dictates outcomes. The material presence of time is everywhere in the first love story: clocks, do-or-die deadlines, the use of the freeze frame and expiration dates on cans of pineapple appear as visual markers throughout, littering the landscape – ever reminding the central characters that they will very shortly be out of the time they have been given or have given themselves to do something or for something to happen to them. For Cop 223, once 1 May arrives, 'love' and the likelihood or probability of reconciliation with his girlfriend will have gone (expired like the out-of-date pineapple cans he has used to count down the last few minutes to when, for him, it will finally be over). For the Blonde Woman, her own future will have come to an end on 1 May unless, that is, she pulls off the drug deal. She has in effect been given her own termination date by the drug boss.

In one sense, in the first love story there is an attempt to fix time, to give it 'orders', such as the device of the freeze frame mentioned above, but tellingly, 'time' rarely does what it is told. May doesn't come back, Cop 223 doesn't keep or get the girl, and the Blonde Woman escapes her drug boss, or rather she escapes the 'deadline' that has been given her. In another sense the concept of time is differentiated in terms of whether one just passively waits for something to happen, as is largely the case with Cop 223, moping about, counting down an imaginary, personalised date for his lover's return; or whether one seizes or takes charge of time, as is the case with the Blonde Woman who instigates a surprise, murderous attack on her drug boss so that she can go free.

In the second love story time becomes more abstract, more expansive, and yet even more unwieldy. The central characters are enabled by time: they use it to plan their escapes, their rendezvous' with each other and their life-changing decisions. Faye can live a fantasy life in Cop 663's house because she knows his movements – his *clockwork*-like patterns of behaviour. Faye can reject the time (and place) of the date with Cop 663 at the California bar, and instead can fly off (across different time zones) to the real California, in her new position as flight hostess. But time also buffets the central characters. Once Cop 663 is dumped in the film, he literally 'drifts', echoing or personifying

A man out of time

the very nature of time as it unfolds, unravels and spirals out of control around him. As he waits for Faye in the California bar he is shot in real time in the foreground, while in the background, in fast time, people rush by. The sense that Cop 223 is a man out of time, adrift and at sea, is poetically captured in this shot – he is desperately wishing, hoping that Faye will emerge from the rush and the throng behind him and sit with him for a while, in real/reel time. David Bordwell argues that the film's split structure helps Wong show how time:

> ... shapes the vicissitudes of romance. Part one, with all its expiration dates and ominous digital clocks, is ruled by a single deadline ... Part two stretches over several weeks before providing an epilogue a year after 633's and Faye's aborted date. Without clocks or expiration stamps, the second story makes flight its master metaphor: the toy jet in 633's apartment, the plane that soars overhead, the imagined escape to California, the jokey ways in which the argot of airline travel becomes the language of love, and finally the two boarding passes Faye prepares for 663 – ambivalent Dear John letters. (2000: 286)

All this aesthetic melancholy and dislocation is supported (in both love stories) by the confessional voice-over monologue. Characters are looking back at what might have been; at the cause of events that have led them to recount their lonesome stories in the present. Events, missed opportunities and regrets have in effect already taken place. Their stories are supposedly past tense – they are nostalgic yearnings for that which has already passed. And yet these voice-over monologues are temporally confused. The tense repeatedly changes in these refrains, so that they are often told as if they are still happening, or as a *fait accompli* – as this is what will happen in the future. In short, temporal order is disrupted in the film through these voice-overs, and this is in part compounded by the freeze frame, jump-cut and stretch printing editing techniques which slow down, stop, slice up and extend time, making it seem organic, uneven and circular.

Nonetheless, even for Cop 223, time offers or presents him with a reunion that itself may turn out to be an escape from the personal drift he experiences in the film. One year to the day that Faye abandoned him for 'California', she returns with another 'boarding card' that holds the potential to whisk them both off to this dream destination. Across both stories time brings people together, in seemingly miraculous, chance encounters. For example, Cop 223 just happens to be in the right place at the right time to 'brush' against the Blonde Woman, and then is sitting in the right bar at the right time the exact minute she enters to drown her sorrows nearly 30 days after their faintest of 'contacts'. What are the chances of that? Pretty high in *Chungking Express*.

Chungking Express presents the audience with two love stories out of time. The echoes, parallels and mirrors in the film replace the linearity and cause-and-effect logic found in most mainstream films. Put simply: A plus B does not equal C, in *Chungking Express*. Time is played around with and disrupted in the film so that past, present and future collide. Time, then:

> Has nothing much to do with that of Newtonian physics, linear and uniform ... Its structure is much fuzzier; it draws time zones, zones of turbulence, common to all accidents. One slides more than one moves forward in it, the split between the past and the future is not the consequence of a cut, and the transformation from one to the other could only be described as fluctuating. (Lalanne et al., 1997: 22)

Love is the drug that makes time seem so mixed up: the central characters demand a great deal of time because of their lovesick ways. They demand that it will give them back their girlfriends; hold a special moment forever; give them back things lost to the past. Time is prayed to like it is a God, and like God it only sometimes answers their prayers. Nostalgia for the past is everywhere in the film. But this is a past that may have only happened a few seconds ago. Memories, history, desire, as we shall presently see, are all out of kilter in *Chungking Express*.

A Mise-en-scène of Desire

Chungking Express is a film that is full of beautiful, sensuous images, textures, objects, places and spaces. The Hong Kong cityscape gleams, objects such as compact discs and jukeboxes glitter, and expressionistic reds and blues pour into the street scenes, fast-food joints, hotel rooms and easy bars. One could even argue that the film is good enough to taste/eat, so central is food (and its correlatives, love and desire) to the film's whole visual structure. Cans of pineapple are lovingly bought, lovingly eaten, and lovingly shot as if they hold some magical significance not only to Cop 223 but to the film's message system.

In 'New Hollywood' cinema spectacle is conjured up through breathtaking special effects, pyrotechnics and 'count-down' set-piece action scenarios. In *Chungking Express*, by contrast, spectacle circulates in and around what might be considered more mundane objects such as cans of pineapple, blonde wigs and Western corporate signs such as Coca-Cola and Garfield. A number of these glittering objects are often held in a shot for longer than is narratively necessary, while others are glimpsed, in teasing moments of revelation. The spectacle at the core of *Chungking Express*, then, is one honed in on the surface level nature of everyday objects and ordinary public spaces: objects and spaces that magically take on the mantle of something more profound and meaningful precisely because they are foregrounded with such reverie. But there is something else which is significant about these 'mundane' objects – they are drawn from popular culture so that it is popular culture that gleams in the film, in celebratory gestures and through a web of cohering signifiers. The Blonde Woman best illustrates this: wearing dark shades, a fawn trench coat, full red lipstick and

The Blonde Woman – a conjunction of pop culture signifiers

the blonde wig, she appears as an object of erotic beauty. But she is also noirish, an embodied femme fatale, lifted from the pages of pulp fiction and American films such as *Double Indemnity* (1944); she is a copy or parody of Monroe; and she echoes, so very strikingly, the psycho-killer, transsexual Dr Robert Elliott from Brian De Palma's *Dressed to Kill* (1980).

Nonetheless, this spectacular homage to popular culture can also be considered in the context of the spectacle and the display of consumption. Characters consume popular culture to appear modern, connected and to give (surface) meaning to their faulty, failing lives. The film 'consumes' popular culture to fill its mise-en-scène with desirable objects and subjects and so Hong Kong, in its entirety, appears as a city built on the motor of consumption and services, or as Marchetti puts it:

As an image for contemplation, a stylish, cinematic commodity for consumption. The film makes its surface visible; canted angles, step-printing, slow motion, jump cuts, handheld camera movements, startling ranges of under/overexposure, play with light and filters foreground the technique involved in making the film. It is an object with a surface like the tin of sardines it depicts. It circulates in global markets, perhaps 'speaking' in unexpected ways like the crying dish rag. (2000: 295)

The film, then, not only makes a spectacle out of consumption but also out of the new flow of images produced by modern mass communications. *Chungking Express* is 'made up' from the global trade in corporate signs, goods, services and the (Western) mass media, so that, in effect, it speaks in the visual language of the global village. Travel, movement and transportation are captured in blurry images and expressionistic colours. Western pop songs are often 'played' over imagery that recalls the generic, glossy, MTV pop music video. Cop 223 romances the sleeping Blonde Woman while watching Chinese opera on television. Model Boeing airplanes and Dole pineapple connect the inhabitants to far away places. *Chungking Express* radiates beauty and energy in and through the objects, sites and practices of the global economy. The film 'strives to haul cinema out of the cinema, to connect it to different sites, those carrying the large flows of new images, of audio-visual and of virtual reality' (Lalanne et al.,1997: 14).

But the film offers the spectator a mise-en-scène of desire in another, more complicated sense. Desire, affection and personal commitment are communicated in and through these consumption objects and sites. Cop 223 demonstrates his love for the girl who has dumped him through eating his way through her favourite food, tins of pineapple. It is as if by eating them he is in effect being with(in) her. When the

Korean shop owner refuses to sell him near out-of-date tins of pineapples, Cop 223 accuses him of not respecting or recognising the 'feelings' of the tins. These 'feelings', of course, have been transposed from the girl into the tins – so that when the tins are thrown out, his love will also have been thrown away, disposed of. Faye fills Cop 663's apartment with foods, goods, CDs and new clothes because she (believes she) is getting closer to him, getting to know him more intimately, through these taste distinctions and personal choices. For all intents and purposes Faye imagines that they are having a commodity inflected relationship with one another. In one sense Cop 663 is implicated in this commodity/space love affair, although his 'romance of goods' (Marchetti, 2002) is for another girl. He believes the changes that are taking place in his flat are because the flat is mourning his break-up with his air hostess girlfriend. When the flat floods it is because it is grief-stricken for his dearly missed ex-girlfriend.

One can read this vision of love projected in and through the (global) commodity in two contrasting ways. First, the possibility of real, lasting intimacy seems to have been effaced by the glittering aura of the commodity sign. So ingrained, so central are these goods to the way the characters make meaning out of their everyday lives that they become the motor or catalyst for all their decisions, including who/how they should fall in love. The characters only seem able to find comfort, nurture, safety in these throw-away goods, and yet it is only through their possession, their control, that they seem best able to communicate their true feelings. But like the goods themselves, these feelings seem fleeting or at least transient, unable to properly root or take effect precisely because they are based on objects whose value perishes rapidly. Characters change their partners just like they change goods that have lost their shine. One can argue, then, that

Chungking Express presents a vision of intimacy haunted by an aching sense of loneliness. The characters seem frightened by real flesh-to-flesh intimacy – Faye runs away from Cop 663 when the chance of a 'real' relationship emerges – precisely because they have grown up in a culture where technological mediation, flux, hi-rate consumption and travel are the material out of which they are defined.

Alternatively, however, one can argue that the consumption, exchange and idolisation of goods, as metaphors of love and romance, actually work to present a vision of intimacy between people that is far more charged, far more vital than ones based on more traditional notions of courtship. These commodity-inflected relationships are often presented as if the advertising jargon that so often accompanies these goods has so filled them up with romantic, exotic, erotic meaning, that they are pregnant with affection, and this affection is recognised by all the parties concerned. A tin of pineapple, then, is much more a sign of goodness, of healthy living, of shared tastes, of juicy intimacy – it is as close to great, fast sex as one can get. What these goods do is actually increase the intimacy between characters, not lessen them – they fill the world with glitter and with gold. Or do they?

The Sounds of Loneliness

Chungking Express is not only a visual exploration of time, love and romance, but a sonic one too. The film makes metaphoric use of dialogue, the voice-over monologue and diegetic music, to accentuate the rhyme and rhythm of the narrative, to concretise the sense of transience and flow, and to add 'biographical' detail to the central characters. As David Martinez suggests:

The intrinsic complementarity between sound-world and story is probably what makes it possible to watch Wong Kar-wai's films many times over without becoming bored. Each one works like a piece of music, with a refrain, repeats, and a catchy tune. They establish Wong Kar-wai as the inventor of a new form of cinema, the musical chronicle, which differs from the musical itself principally in that the actors do not sing (at least, not on stage). (Lalanne et al., 1997: 35)

In *Chungking Express*, a particular musical metre emerges through both the dialogue between characters and (particularly) the voice-over monologue. Lines are delivered with melancholic introspection and with all the lyrical sensitivity of a soliloquy or a poetic couplet. Meaning hangs on not just what is said but also the way it is said. Cop 223's pining for his girlfriend achieves its register through the slow, deliberate, delivery of lines that seem to have been forever in the making, like those memories he wants to last forever. For example, he says, 'If memories could be canned, would they also have expiration dates? If so, I hope they last for centuries'. These lines score his aching heart like violins are actually playing in the fine rasps of the words. Tone, intonation and timbre fuse to haul the lines into the same sonic field as the pop music that so often emerges to add further texture to the themes in play. In fact, one can argue that some kind of music finds its way into every crevice in the film, so that the film 'sings' its proclamations of lost love and sensuous intimacy.

Music or a particular song is often used to reveal and explain the deepest yearnings of a character. Faye's strong desire to flee Hong Kong is foregrounded through the use of two tracks: The Mamas and the Papas' 'California Dreaming', and a Cantopop version of The Cranberries' 'Dreams' (sung by the actress, Faye Wong). Both songs suggest that Faye is a dreamer, more content, complete, when she has transported herself to the places and spaces referenced in the two songs. So while she works at the Midnight Express, and as she goes about cleaning Cop 663's flat, these songs fill the screen space, allowing her to 'time travel', to move across the borders that she so feels so hemmed in by. In fact, these songs may very well be the influence or catalyst for wanting to go somewhere else in the first place – it is as if they have provided an alternative utopian universe for her to go and exist in, and, of course, not being there is tearing her apart. The air hostess who jilts Cop 663 also has her own song, Dinah Washington's 'What a Difference a Day Makes'. Sung for the first time when the two are making out in his apartment, it very quickly becomes a prophetic cue for their separation – articulating the film's central theme that nothing can stay the same, and 24 hours is actually a long time for major changes to happen in.

Dialogue, voice-overs and pop music work in another way in the film: they again draw attention to the 'global village' that the characters find themselves living in, highlighting the profusion of world sounds that wire Hong Kong. Cop 223 speaks a heavily accented Cantonese, something he has got from Taiwan schooling. But he also seamlessly switches from Cantonese to English to Japanese to Mandarin depending on whom he is talking to. The Blonde Woman speaks an English accented Mandarin, but she also uses English to converse with the Indian drug mules. Characters let – or cannot help but let – language slip and slide precisely because, in the global context of Hong Kong, no one language is connected to any one singular identity. In fact, finding a common language to communicate in is part of the contemporary condition: language, then, has its own varied menu in *Chungking Express*. The pop music confirms this sense of a global culture blaring its way into the Hong Kong psyche – and in promising green leaves and sunny beaches, America itself appears as the sonic and iconic beacon of a new world order of plenitude.

Although, finally, the film suggests that this representation may well be illusory. Faye has no doubt seen a great many movies and adverts that have shown California as a utopian space. Faye has no doubt dreamed-up this space, fantasising about what it would be like to live there, as she sings along to 'California Dreaming'. But when she arrives, one suspects that the real disappoints in relation to the imagined, and she returns to the Midnight Express, lonely, looking for the one man who may in the end be able to make her dreams come true.

3. Representation

Lonely Men and Absent Families

In *Chungking Express* one arguably finds an identity crisis in relation to the representation of both the men and women found in the film. This is an identity crisis that leaves all the central characters floundering, unsure of their masculinity, femininity or societal 'role'. For them, Hong Kong has become a city where the rules around social relationships and identity formation have been blurred and seriously undermined by new global realities in consumption, travel and communication. In *Chungking Express*, Hong Kong's ethnic hybridity is in part responsible for such existential flux. In this desperately over-crowded city one can meet and greet almost any 'culture' from anywhere in the world. People come and go, literally and metaphorically, as travellers, immigrants, and refugees. Transnational businessmen holiday there, escape from their normal routines there, and sell their commodities and stocks there, making lots of money in the process. Open all the time, with little green spaces, one is caught in a bewildering malaise of people, signs, goods, services and languages. In *Chungking Express*, the city is too fast, too full of (different) people on the move, and the aura of the commodity and the consumption of the brand have come to dominate social life. Characters choose brands instead of one another, or they make life decision changes on the basis of the brands that they try, or they dream of finding happiness in far off spaces that they will have first seen in an advert or a film or a pop video. Tins of pineapple, fish and chips, contraband, and American pop songs are engines of and for many of the key decisions made in the film. For example, Cop 223 laments that to May 'I am just another can of pineapple'. Marchetti suggests that:

Commodities – culturally mediated, tainted, fetishistic

certainly, but concrete – remain the most certain conduit for the communication of personal feelings and desires. To get to know the blonde drug trafficker (whom he never knows), Cop 223 asks if she likes pineapple (in several languages). Cop 663 recognises and expresses his feelings for Faye by returning the compact disk of the Mamas and Papas tunes he had mistaken earlier as a gift from his ex-girlfriend. (2002: 304)

But communication is filtered in another way in *Chungking Express*. Instead of characters communicating face-to-face with each other, they choose telecommunications, such as pagers; they use symbols such as the boarding pass; or they use the voice-over monologue, when no one else is there – as if communicating with 'shadows' or 'ghosts' is easier (more like modern life itself) than the real thing. This failure in interpersonal communication is particularly true of the male characters. Both Cop 223 and 663 struggle to communicate with other people, particularly women; they find it difficult to understand the fast changing cultures around them, they feel unable to control the trajectory (destiny) of their lives, and they fail to keep the interest (or commitment) of their female love interests. In one sense they are presented as weak, ineffectual men who fail to act and who only speak when it is too late. The poetry found in the voice-over monologues, and the obsessive commitments to things that stand in for their love, only take effect when the love interest has gone. According to Marchetti, both Cops are emblematic of 'a crisis in the authority of patriarchy and in traditional notions of masculinity' (ibid.: 307). Both Cops have become too feminine, too domesticated, too nurturing and loving. Cop 223 cleans the Blonde Woman's shoes while she sleeps, and he acts like the punch-drunk heroine of romantic pulp fiction, weeping over his lost lover. Cop 663 is identified with the domestic space of his flat, engaging in melancholic conversations with towels and walls. Both Cops are also 'beautiful' to look at, physically androgynous, and they hold the gaze as much, if not more than, the female characters in the film. As such they become objects of erotic beauty, on show, in the same way as a glittering bottle of beer or a bejewelled city street. Given that both Cops are symbols of penal authority, then it is law and order which is itself feminised, and given that the 'hard bodied' Blonde Woman is literally on the other side of law, power itself seems to be in flux, oscillating between men and women in the film.

The female characters are also affected by the instability in and blurring of gender norms. In *Chungking Express*, for the most part, men can no longer measure up to them, or up to the commodities and media fantasies that fill their cultural world and which they seem intimately connected to. In this context, one can offer a different interpretation of the reason why Faye fills Cop 663's flat with the objects, clothes and goods of her choosing. This will allow her to create a fantasy space and a 'fantasy' man to share it with. It is not because she obsesses over the 'real' Cop 663 – this is clear when she runs away from him when he catches her there – rather she uses the flat to give materiality to the fantasies of heterosexual love that circulate in her head. He can never eclipse – be as good as – the man in her dreams.

The female characters also seem to be able to exercise a greater freedom, and a greater degree of control over their lives. According to Marchetti, the new service and commodity based economy has given women economic freedom and opened up choices about the way they live their lives:

All the women in the film fly off (in the cases of the drug trafficker, the stewardess, and Faye, quite literally in

airplanes) and leave the men to fend for themselves. Officially (on the police force) or economically (as small businessmen), the men are grounded, while the women move freely in he new service (airline hostess) and informal (drug trafficking) parts of the global economy. (2002: 307)

But the women also suffer terrifying fractured subjectivities in the film. None of the central female characters are happy with whom they are, and for the most part they all walk around in some sort of disguise or uniform, pretending to be complete, or hiding from who they really are. The Blonde Woman is the best example of this: the dark shades, trench coat and Monroe wig allow her to 'perform' the role of the femme fatale, and in a city full of such global references, she fits in better than if she was stripped of these icons. The Blonde Woman lives out this fantasy role but is obviously tired of it – it is not her, it is mere representation – and it is this mask that she is running away from in the film. This is a mask probably given to her by the drugs boss – we see him with a simulacrum of her (another Asian woman in a blonde wig) just moments before she kills him – as if she has been his fetishistic construction all along. When she throws the wig away near the end of he first love story, she is revealing her inner core, but of course, in a Hong Kong with a penchant for popular culture, this may actually mean that she will be more out of place than ever.

All this identity crisis and fractured subjectivity is compounded by a number of distancing techniques employed by Wong Kar-wai; as already noted there is little action, and little direct communication between characters. The film is actually marked by a great deal of silence, of things not being said, or of sentences not being fully completed. All the central characters are and remain enigmas. Marchetti argues that this is one of the central reasons why *Chungking Express* has close associations with European Art Cinema:

The characters found in *Chungking Express* do not present themselves as the traditionally unified creations of classical Hollywood. Rather, these sometimes nameless, sometimes faceless, creations are closer to Brecht's or Godard's characters. (2002: 291)

There are no fathers, mothers or children in *Chungking Express*: in effect the traditional nuclear and extended family has disappeared from the Hong Kong landscape, and with it the familial ties that usually bind people together. At their loneliest, their most despairing, neither cop, nor the Blonde Woman, have anyone to turn to, no 'home' space to set foot in. It as if all the central characters are orphans, or cannot communicate with their kin because relationships have sometime ago (somehow) broken down. They take their counselling from pineapples, fish and chips and beer. Cop 223 spends his birthday with a complete stranger. Faye is able to 'fly off' presumably because she is free of ties. The Blonde Woman throws away her wig and exits right (out of the film) with little more than a look over her shoulder.

One can also read the absence of the family in allegorical terms: Hong Kong is an orphan or a bastard child – its parentage uncertain – with Britain, China and the amorphous 'global culture' with claims to its birthright. Hong Kong will soon be orphaned again, with Britain giving up its 'foster child' to China, Hong Kong's legitimate (but unsuitable) 'parents'. In a foreboding sign, this future is one without children, as if Hong Kong will itself cease to be, unable to reproduce the vision of itself, once it is handed over 1997. (1)

Hong Kong as an Allegorical Place

1 July 1997

Chungking Express can be read as an expression of the fears surrounding Hong Kong's return to China on July 1997. One can discuss the film's obsession with time, flight, loss and abandonment in terms of the 'meltdown' that the city was experiencing in the run up to succession. One can revisit the motifs, themes and metaphors so far discussed in this guide, then, and see a story of Hong Kong emerge that is touched or tainted by this political reality.

In this interpretation of the film, the two love stories become a device to express the belief that Hong Kong was itself being abandoned, cut adrift or 'jilted', without the means to protect itself or negotiate its own 'separation'. Cop 223 and Cop 663, connected to the formal institutions of power in Hong Kong, can do nothing to keep their lovers, or satisfy their lovers – they are ineffectual or powerless to stop, halt or reverse this loss – they just can't hold the centre together. They are merely foot soldiers that are taken charge of. In this context, the film presents Hong Kong as a city that is worth preserving. In fact, one can argue that there is another love affair in the film: one with Hong Kong itself, and so the sensuous intimacy in the film is one borne out of a longing for the Hong Kong that is but very soon won't be. When things, objects, people weep in the film they are weeping for Hong Kong.

Hong Kong is abandoned in another way in the film: by the very people who populate it. The flight metaphor in the film can be read as a sign of a mass exodus, of people leaving in droves because of the impending hand-over. The signifiers of flight are everywhere in the film; airports, travel, migration, model Boeing airplanes, boarding passes and the escapist lyrics in pop songs that provide a great deal of the soundtrack.

Even when Faye returns from a year away (a yearning return to the beautiful city, rather than to Cop 663?) she plans to leave again, and perhaps to take Cop 663 with her. The job she has as an air hostess couldn't be more apt for a city trying to escape its future. By contrast, in comparison, China appears as a suffocating regime – an expiration date – that will extinguish the freedoms that Hong Kong presently has. As Marchetti argues, *Chungking Express*:

> **Plays up the transnational/transcultural associations that point to a cosmopolitan, urban culture in keeping with the perception of Mainland China as monolithic, isolated, 'primitive', and out of the swing of the global economy. (2002: 293)**

If one isn't in 'flight' in *Chungking Express* then one is on the run. Part of the film's breathless intoxication is created through people running and being chased. The metaphor of the chase, of pursuit, of running away (from someone/something) is also something that works across both love stories, and can be connected to the allegorical reading that Hong Kong is itself on-the-run (from China). The film opens with Cop 223 chasing a criminal; the Blonde Woman chases the Indians who have betrayed her, and is in turn chased by the drug boss's henchmen; and Faye runs away from Cop 663 when he finds her in his flat. In all the active chase/pursuit scenes, movement, speed and rush are more generally captured through the way the crowds are shot. Shot in fast-time, faceless people race across the scene, mere blobs of colour and shade, chased by 'demons' that have no material present in the film, but which come from the collective psyche or imagination of a people looking over their shoulder – at China, perhaps, just across the water. Chase, of course, defines the nature of love in the film: Cop 223 'chases' his girlfriend; Faye first 'chases' Cop 663 and is then actively pursued by him. In *Chungking Express* even love is on the run.

The passing of time and the setting of deadlines are also central to the way the film foregrounds the

The metaphor of the chase is central to Chungking Express

perception that an unstoppable 'countdown' is taking place: all the references to time, all the devices of time that appear in the film, put the characters (the city) on a collision course with their hopes, wishes and desires. Cop 223 counts down the date to 1 May hoping that his girlfriend will come back to him before the clock turns its last second over to his self-imposed deadline. The Blonde Woman moves closer to her own 'expiration' date, and Dinah Washington sings 'what a difference a day makes, 24 little hours', cementing the sense that change (death) is going to come whatever.

Although, not entirely. The Blonde Woman doesn't die in the film, but instead turns the deadline on her drug boss by killing him. She does stop her own expiration date and re-defines her identity as well – throwing her blonde wig away, perhaps reconnecting herself to Hong Kong in the process. Hong Kong may survive then, but compromises – a change in style and outlook – will have to take place. As the Blonde Woman herself laments, change is all a part of being human.

Any-Space-Whatever

The ephemeral places and spaces the characters visit in

Chungking Express, situated as they are within a city that is itself transient, and without a fixed centre, function as 'any-space-whatevers'. Deleuze, who adapts the term from the French anthropologist Pascal Augé, defines an 'any-space-whatsoever' as a space such as a metro stop, a doctor's waiting room or an airport terminal. It is an anonymous space people pass through, a point of transit between places of 'importance', such as the metro, which is merely the space one passes through between home and work. Deleuze considers the 'any-space-whatever' as a condition for the emergence of uniqueness and singularities. The anonymity of space gives rise to an infinite possibility of creation. Deleuze suggests that:

> **'Any-space-whatever is not an abstract universal, in all times, in all places. It is a perfectly singular space, which has merely lost its homogeneity, that is, the principle of its metric relations or the connection of its own parts, so that the linkages can be made in an infinite number of ways. It is a space of virtual conjunction, grasped as pure locus of the possible' (1989: 113).**

Anything is possible in *Chungking Express*: the arteries and veins of the bars, fast food joints and neon-lit shops enable the characters to drift in and out of time, in and out of space, so that they are not held, finally, in the grip of rational time and ordered materiality. The folds and flow of time, the multiplicities in every inch of space, open up the image to innumerable spectatorial opportunities.

The Global in the Local

Chungking Express can be argued to be a film that explicitly deals with the way globalisation has affected or transformed the way people experience, communicate and form identities in the local spaces of their cities or neighbourhoods. The modern mass media, new media technologies, including the Internet, and the trade in global goods and services, have all supposedly had a profound effect on everyday local life. No longer is any space, place or 'culture' separate, in fact the contrary is true: every space, place and 'culture' is interconnected, creating what has been termed the global village, or as Marshal Mcluhan eloquently puts it:

After three thousand years of explosion, by means of fragmentary and mechanical technologies, the Western world is imploding. During the mechanical ages we had extended our bodies in space. Today, after more than a century of electric technology we have extended our central nervous system itself in a global embrace, abolishing both space and time as far as our planet is concerned ... As electrically contracted, the globe is no more than a village. (1989: 32)

Through cultural globalisation, people's everyday experiences of the world have been fundamentally changed because of the transmission of the images, lifestyles *and* commodities of a diverse number of world cultures into 'local' homes, work places, public networks and leisure spaces. In these global/local encounters, space and time are 'uncoupled' because there is no longer a linear connection between where a person is physically and where a person can actually be symbolically transported to. Through the objects, sites and images of global culture, a second-hand 'travel' experience emerges without one necessarily having to travel. People in Hong Kong can, for example, experience the 'culture' of America through the pop video/song, film blockbuster, designer clothes, fast-food, convenience foods, cars, postcards that can be found on their high streets, on television and at the cinema, in the bars, cafes and restaurants, and in their homes. One can clearly see the expression, the interrogation of the effects of global culture on the local in *Chungking Express*.

In one sense, the film pays homage to American films, music, brands and goods. Rather than there just being a romance of goods, then, there is a romance of American culture. Film noir, California, Coca-Cola, Garfield, Monroe, Boeing planes, Pan Am uniforms, Caesar Salads and tins of pineapple herald the centrality of America to the way people consume, live and give identity to themselves. Faye is so in love with the representation of California that she up and leaves; Cop 223 is so in love with (American) pineapples that he eats them until he is sick; *the film* is so in love with American films that it apes the voice-over monologue and inflects the *femme fatale* of the American film noir.

In another sense, *Chungking Express* comments critically on this (American) cultural invasion, and suggests that simulacra (copy, imitation, the second-hand experience of America) are eroding the authenticity of Hong Kong. In this reading of the film, Hong Kong is running out of time because of this 'Western' swamping, and not because of the looming hand-over to China. Cultural globalisation is seen to produce a *deterritorisation* experience. This can be defined as the loss of the 'natural' relation of culture to its physical and geographical point of origin – precisely because cultural texts begin to 'free float' or circulate in the global sphere. What communication technologies and global capitalism create is the erosion of cultural borders and local-cultural boundaries, and with it, arguably, local-cultural distinctiveness.

What is arguably being played out in *Chungking Express* is the fear of cultural homogenisation. As the characters in the film all begin to meet and greet the same range of cultural texts on a daily basis they become seduced by their utopian sentiments and promises of a good, happy life. They feel compelled to buy into them, perhaps at the expense of their own local traditions, arts and practices. Faye has fallen in love with American culture and as a consequence there is nothing from Hong Kong that can satisfy her. The fear at the heart of the film, then, becomes one of cultural standardisation, a standardisation based on the dream networks and fantasies produced and imposed by the Western media, and in particular, the America media. In this respect, Marchetti concludes that:

> The local is poured into molds that can no longer be located in the East or West, Third or First World's, periphery or center. For example, the Garfield toy and the boom boxes in the shop display are probably manufactured in China, designed by American or Japanese films, bought and sold in entrepots like Hong Kong and finally used by a cosmopolitan consumer. In this vein, it seems fitting that the film should end with a shot of the portable stereo at the deli. The transnationals – whether JVC, Sony, or Motorola – have the last word. (2002: 303)

John Thompson (1995) argues that globalisation has a dramatic effect on the way people experience the world. Globalisation produces a situation of 'mediated worldliness', where people's understanding and knowledge of the world are increasingly shaped by the mediated symbolic forms they encounter. Western films, music videos, documentaries and television/print news are the reality checks that people use to make sense of the world, and these, it is argued are never neutral, never accurate. Faye yearns for California because of what she has seen and heard about it through the mass media. For her, or rather for The Mamas and Papas, it is a utopian space – warm, sunny, existentially free. The Blonde Woman dresses like she has watched (taken in) too many American films, and both cops are not that far removed from the world-weary 'Dicks' of American pulp fiction. However, these 'instances' of American culture are all shown to ultimately disappoint. When Faye finally gets to California it clearly does not meet her expectations, and she returns home, to re-ignite her romance with Hong Kong/Cop 663. The Blonde Woman rids herself of her American disguise the first moment that she can. Cop 223 gets sick of American culture and gives up on this particular romance. The film has a love/hate relationship with American culture and is, finally, clearly more ambiguous about the effect of global culture on its characters and on its spaces.

Chungking Express's population mirrors that of Hong Kong. In its city numerous ethnic cultures, backgrounds and histories interconnect and fuse. Hong Kong has always been a heterogeneous melting pot – it has always been an interconnected global village, and one finds evidences of this everywhere. Languages mix and collide; dress styles, fashion, foods and goods take the spectator to the four corners of the world. *Chungking Express*'s visual beauty emerges from the sights, sounds, smells and buildings of this divergent metropolis. The global in the local is not 'new' to Hong Kong, but just to the rest of the world.

(A Celebration of) Postmodernism

Postmodern theory attempts to understand what are seen as radical transformations in the way people live and understand the world they live in – transformations that are argued to have been in large part motored by new media technologies and transnational capitalism. It is argued that through the twentyfourseven consumption of film, video and television, the multi-media 'text', the virtual reality of the Internet and electronic gaming devices, and through the world-wide trade in global branded goods and services, the way people experience 'reality' has been fundamentally altered. In effect, what is being suggested here is that in a postmodern world, the real (reality) has been turned upside down or inside out so that virtual encounters in mediated environments (such as the cinema, themed restaurant, theme park, shopping mall and disco) are where people increasingly live their lives. In a postmodern world, the 'natural' and the 'authentic' are only experienced second-hand (via remote control, branded good, themed space, computer mouse or gaming console) and people seem to prefer the risk-free fantasy and the plenitude of these simulated environments.

Chungking Express not only critically explores the idea of the 'second-hand' experience but also itself seems to be postmodern in style, design and execution. The film is full of virtual or themed encounters. Cop 223 continues his affair with his girlfriend through (in) tins of pineapple and makes 'first contact' conversation with the Blonde Woman by asking her if she likes pineapples. His romance of her is *only virtual*: while she sleeps he watches Chinese opera on television and then he consummates their relationship through cleaning her shoes. They are never actually closer than 0.01cm as if touch would itself be too 'real' or too authentic for them. She says goodbye not with a kiss but with a paged 'happy birthday' message. Faye has a totally simulated relationship with Cop 663, transforming his apartment with goods, brands, clothes and CDs of her choice. She dreams of California as it is represented in song and image, changing her occupation so that she can visit the place of her dreams (and not in effect the 'real' California at all). In *Chungking Express* the characters meet in simulated environments, such as the 'themed bar' California. Even the low-rent Chungking Mansions seems to be a 'tourist' inspired representation, with all the clichés of marketplace, flop house, sweat shop and textiles self-consciously present.

In *Chungking Express*, the world appears to shrink: space and time differences conflate, as all the (simulated) cultures of the globe circulate there. Life in the city is intoxicating but disorientating, and the film captures this sense of implosion through its non-linear narrative structure and anti-realist editing techniques. The story meanders, arcs and echoes back on itself, full of its own imitation and repetition. Three of the four central characters appear in both stories; the metaphors and instances of time are found repeating themselves across both stories; the places or palaces of consumption are doubled up, most notably with the Midnight Express; and the sad refrains of lost love and the recanting of existential philosophy 'haunt' both stories.

Time and space itself are called into question in the film; through the use of the freeze frame, time stops in the film; through the use of the hand-held camera, subjectivity appears shaky; and through the use of the jump-cut and stretch-print, action and motivation are 'cut up' and dislocated, as if the characters are adrift in this sea of instantaneous commodity gratification. In the film's opening sequence, Cop 223 is chasing a criminal through what are busy streets, dripping in colour and awash with neon electrification. While he is shot in focus, the background is a blur, a moving quilt of smudges. However, for one moment, time stops, through the device of the freeze frame, and focuses on the ultimate commodity fetish: the 'made' up femme fatale, the Blonde Woman. He immediately falls in love with her – a mere *representation* of a woman from a film genre made 40 years previously.

Janice Tong makes sense of the relationship between time and space, and media technology by arguing that *Chungking Express* shows Hong Kong to be:

> **A compressed space that forces its people to make physical contact with one another without making any connections, even effecting disconnections from their selves. Just as the city and its citizens embrace time in the express speed of communication via mobile phones, emails, faxes, so too these technologies elicit distance and displacement between people. (2003: 52)**

In *Chungking Express*, this 'displacement between people' refers one to another postmodern trope: that of individual and cultural schizophrenia. The postmodern condition produces people (and spaces) who are 'split', who have more than one identity or personality. In *Chungking Express* none of the central characters know who they are or how they should behave, and they are all, to a degree, in disguise. Both Cops hide behind their police uniforms; the Blonde Woman hides behind her wig and sunglasses; the voice-over monologue allows both Cops to play out a different role to the one that is presented in flesh and bone, that of world weary, eloquent romantic; the characters switch between different languages as if they are flitting between different identities; and Faye escapes into the air hostess uniform to become the epitome of American cool. The film, then, presents us with a postmodern crisis in identity formation: with so many identities now on offer (in this postmodern menu of life), the borders and boundaries of masculinity, femininity, ethnicity and nationality all break down. And this is potentially terrifying for all concerned.

One way in which the film captures this sense of individual and cultural confusion is through the blocked, the partial and

Reflected images capture the confusion of the individual

the 'mirrored' vision. *Chungking Express* is full of reflected images of and from the central characters, with mirrors and windows the dominant framing device. Faye, the Blonde Woman, Cop 223 and Cop 663 are all caught looking at each other through mirrors (in hotel rooms, restaurants and bars) and windows – a strategy that multiplies their 'selfs' and distances them from the real spaces that they are found in. Characters also appear only partially in the frame, obscured by objects, goods and the interiors of buildings. They appear incomplete, fractured, without existential plentitude, in a city itself caught in a gaze that only partially recognises its history/identity.

Chungking Express is also full of the indicators of cultural schizophrenia: Hong Kong is a mish-mash of so many different identities that it has no centre, no inner, stable core, and this is played out in the film through the goods, brands, people and sounds that populate the narrative. The film is often full of bewildering, filtered images, reflections, sounds and dislocated film cuts precisely because it is attempting to capture a warehouse of contradictory influences and impulses. However, this schizophrenia extends to the way past, present and future tense are upset in the film. *Chungking Express* is full of the signs of an American culture that has already passed: the Pan Am uniforms and model Boeing planes are actually drawn from Wong Kar-wai's childhood; the two central tracks by the Mamas and Papas and Dinah Washington are from the same period; and even the ubiquitous Coca-Cola and Garfield have their reference points in advertising campaigns and comic series that had their heyday in the late 1960s and early 1970s. Of course, the intertextual reference points to film noir confuse the film's sense of history even more, and this, finally, is compounded by the connections to Godard's work with the French New Wave. If *Chungking Express* is Wong Kar-wai's *A bout de souffle*, then there is a nostalgic yearning for a film form from a long, long time ago. *Chungking Express* is decidedly postmodern because it exhibits, to appropriate Brooker and Brooker's understanding of Fredric Jameson's definition of it:

> **A formal self-consciousness, borrowing from other texts and styles in a meta-historical and cross generic free-for-all which breaks down distinctions between high and low, Western and other cultures, or the past and present. (Brooker and Brooker, 1997: 3)**

Postmodern accounts of the new media and global culture are generally apocalyptic in nature: together they strip away the very basis of what it means to be human, transforming the world into mediated and simulated environments where branded copies of everything fire the way people live and the way people understand the way they live. As Baudrillard writes, 'now the media are nothing else than a marvelous instrument for destabilising the real and the true' (quoted in Poster, 1988: 217). In *Chungking Express*, however, there is much more of an ambivalent understanding or exploration of postmodernism. In one sense, this is because Hong Kong's unique identity is one that is dependent on the signs, symbols and themes of postmodernity: its multi-racial, consumption driven interior, and its place as a city caught between East and West, are what make it so unique. In fact, one could argue that there is actually a yearning for, a celebration of displacement, convergence, speed and simulation in the film. A celebration, then, of the sensuous intimacy of postmodernism, where cans of pineapple radiate out like an epiphany moment.

4. Textual Analysis

Close textual analysis is perhaps the only way that one can really get to the 'inner skin' of a film. Through completely 'undressing' a 2–5 minute sequence, for example, one is engaging with all the formal, aesthetic and thematic mechanisms/strategies that are used to make a film meaningful, enjoyable and ideological. Good textual analysis requires the 'reader' to pay close attention to the film's narrative, the characterisation, the editing, the soundscape, the setting and lighting, and representation (of gender, class, race, sexuality and nationality). When one begins to read a film sequence like this, one should have a mental checklist of all the things to look out for, so that in turn the full glory of the sequence emerges, piece by piece, slowly but surely.

One could take almost any 2 minutes from *Chungking Express* and explore or mine them to discover the rich complexities of meaning which can be found in the film. From the very first moment of the film, in fact, the viewer is thrust into a world of innovative cinematography, complex and fragmentary narration, and enigmatic, highly charged characters who measure their lives in terms of expiry dates, fast-food and the distant dreams of far-off places. Through the close textual analysis of the opening 2 minutes of *Chungking Express* one immediately gets a sense of the film's formal style, its narrative trajectory, its thematic concerns and its revolutionary place within national and international cinema. *Chungking Express* starts as if it is *dressed to kill*.

Dressed To Kill

The opening 2 minutes to *Chungking Express* are explosive. The film literally and metaphorically starts 'on the run'. The opening hand-held 'establishing shot' of a chaotic street scene captures the Blonde Woman on the move. She enters the film from the right, almost walking into the camera as it tracks her movement through the street. A high degree of subjectivity is immediately created: the 'roaming' camera is given human qualities, as if it were also one of the faceless people in the shot. The images in this shot are blurred, smudged and time has been slowed down so although people are rushing madly by they move slowly across the frame, like spectres or ghosts. A series of oscillating looks are quickly established. The camera looks at the Blonde Woman, the Blonde Woman looks at the crowd, and the blurred faces in the shot also make fleeting eye-contact with the camera. This brings a high degree of self-reflexivity or self-consciousness to the shot but also, in narrative terms, a degree of paranoia – as if all the people, and the Blonde Woman in particular, are worried that they are being followed – and given the way the camera has functioned in this opening shot, this sense of paranoia is given some justification. It is as if the audience has entered the film at the point where either an illicit, dangerous rendezvous is about to take place, or that 'someone' is or thinks that they are, being followed.

The Blonde Woman is a striking figure: dressed in dark glasses, a long rain-coat and with bright red lips she looks like she has walked straight out of a Hollywood movie. Coded as a femme fatale, and given the energy of the shot, she looks like she is herself on the run, and so the exchange of glances cements the sense that 'pursuit' is going to be central to the film's diegesis. The thumping, part-whining electronic music that scores the shot(s) adds to the tension, and in terms of spectatorship, sets the pulses racing. This is compounded by the diegetic street noises that begin to bang out a constant dull rhythm, and which sit just beneath the musical score.

The camera looks at the Blonde Woman...

...who looks at the faces in the crowd...

...who look back at her.

The next, rapidly cut together, series of moving, hand-held shots, continue the skewed subjectivity of the first shot. At one moment the audience is presented with what seems to be a point of view shot from the Blonde Woman's perspective, and yet she suddenly appears in the same shot. The kinetic movement of the camera through the blue-filtered, grubby, crowded public spaces of trading and gambling, fill the shots with 'nameless' faces, many of whom take time to stare at the Blonde Woman/ the camera as she/it breezes past. These shots are hyper-busy, claustrophobic in their density, and they are also disorientating. Through the use of the jump-cut, the Blonde

Woman's movement is consistent (in time) but inconsistent (in space). She floats over the materiality of the shot rather like a ghost. The suggested 'direct address' is also disconcerting. In the very first few seconds of the film, the viewer is caught in the gaze of people whose faces are almost smudged out of existence.

Chungking Express starts, then, with many of its thematic and stylistic devices in place. One can already read this opening as allegorical. Hong Kong is on the run from China, and its inhabitants could very well be effaced out of history. People are leaving in droves and so the city itself is being filled with ghosts, or will very soon only have the ghosts of memories to reconcile its past. The paranoia present is political: very soon Hong Kong will be invaded, taken over by Mainland China. The themes of consumption, globalisation are also present – we enter the film at the level of commerce, and with a high degree of racial heterogeneity (we could in fact very well be in 'India' given the racial coding of the people in the shots.). Stylistically, the codes and conventions of European Art Cinema are present. The subversion of or play with subjectivity, the discontinuity editing techniques, and the high degree of self-reflexivity mark the film out as contemplative, dislocated, as radically different from the (Hollywood) mainstream. And yet, Hollywood is also centre stage right from the off, in the form of the Blonde Woman. She is a Monroe muse, a film noir femme fatale and the transsexual psycho-killer from Brian De Palma's *Dressed to Kill.*

In the long trench-coat that could be hiding a weapon, she is, cinematically speaking, dressed to kill (although given the implication of her being a sexual(ised) woman, she could also be dressed to be killed). As she enters a chrome reflecting lift, to start the next quick succession of shots, the '*homage*' to the film *Dressed to Kill* is explicit and exact. She mirrors or resembles, so very closely, the murderous Dr. Robert Elliot (Michael Caine) who dresses up in similar attire to slash to death 'monstrous' women. The exterior shot of her in the lift, as the doors slowly close, is lifted straight from this film, and opens up the reading to one that recognises the identity crisis that is also central

The Blonde Woman: an homage to...

...Dressed to Kill and the glittering surface of Hollywood?

to the film's thematic structure. Just as Elliot is in drag in *Dressed to Kill*, the Blonde Woman is in disguise, hiding her real self beneath the signs of Hollywood cinema.

This shot is followed by a rapidly edited sequence of two second shots, as the camera tracks the Blonde Woman (and *becomes* the Blonde Woman) through a maze of long, low key, 'blue' lit, crowded corridors. Most of the faces and bodies that are passed are male/masculine and given the Blonde Woman's (dangerous) beauty the series of looks are tinged with danger and desire. It looks as if she is walking into a trap, entering into an increasingly 'closed' world that could swallow her up at any minute. In one of the shots, she stops dead in her tracks and stares right into the camera that has continued to follow her. The camera/spectator is again implicated in the dynamics of the sequence – made to feel complicit and 'accused' in the 'pursuit' of the Blonde Woman. However, the sequence comes to an abrupt close with her suddenly entering a room and a pair of curtains being drawn behind her. Finally, then, the pursuit/chase/movement motif has been given a degree of closure. She has been expected here, and she enters this space with a high degree of authority. The Blonde Woman is, and was, always in control. The audience have been, to a degree, fooled or have had their viewing position played with in the opening sequence so far. In effect, disorientation is everywhere and this continues as we cut to the title card, 'Chungking Express', before we get to see what is in the room or what the Blonde Woman is really up to.

The shot of the title card is another disruptive device borrowed from European Art Cinema. Just at the exact moment the film should reveal the reason for its enigmatic opening, the audience is taken 'outside' of the film world, to the artifice of cinema itself. This technique is one that is predominately associated with the films of Jean-Luc Godard, and so the breathless momentum of this opening is not that far away from Godard's *A bout de souffle*.

The sequence then continues with what might be called a series of four 'pillow' or abstractly rendered bridging shots, of brooding clouds drifting by on a dull sky. Each shot captures the clouds from a different angle and from a slightly different setting. The first two shots are taken from a roof, with chimneys and TV aerials providing the contrasting lines, shapes and colours to the 'soft' but nonetheless dense clouds that drift by in random (circular) motion. The third and fourth shots are taken from street level, with the ominous looking hi-rises, on three sides of the frame, providing the contrast: black brick to rolling cloud. The shots of the clouds are highly metaphoric. They add semiotic weight to the idea of transience, of movement, of transformation and change that is so central to the opening sequence, and to the film in its entirety. Nothing can stop the clouds' movement and as we shall later see in the film, nothing will stop relationships breaking down. The clouds, then, are one of the first devices of time in the film. But they are also metaphoric in another sense: they are represented in stark contrast to the vertical and horizontal lines of 'man-made' objects and buildings, the natural as opposed to the manufactured or constructed. The clouds also act as a pathetic fallacy: these full clouds promise rain, they foreshadow the tears and the floods that will pour out of the star-crossed lovers in the film.

Of course, the pillow shots can be read as perfect-time images, and liquid any-space-whatevers. Through these pillow shots the spectator is offered a pure, unthought form of time, and of transience. Structurally, the uncoupling of temporal and spatial relations set up the formal and thematic concerns of the film.

Over the third shot of the clouds, the device of the voice-over monologue is introduced, and this is again disruptive. Since the title card we have not returned to the 'unfinished' story of the Blonde Woman, and this voice-over appears before the character that speaks it has been given material presence. His ghost, then, hovers over the image of the clouds, themselves ghost-like or at least translucent. We are suddenly in a memory that has already happened, past tense, and nothing can change that. The memories, then, are ghost-like, too. The voice-over monologue also refers the audience back to the private eye in film noir, and so a series of connections are being made back to the 'events' that occurred before the title card appeared. Ghosts hover over both stories, people/things are on the move, and, as we shortly see, 'private eye' 223 is

Nothing can stop the movement of the clouds

Our first glimpse of Cop 223

Cop 223 and the mannequin

destined (or is it luck?) to meet his *femme fatale*.

The first concrete set of shots of Cop 223 also sets up the theme of repetition and relay, and of what might be called the film's circular 'master' narrative. He is also filmed moving along a busy street, but in the opposite direction to the movement of the Blonde Woman that has gone before. The same blurring of the image, and slowing down of the action occurs but this time, brighter, crisper neon lights fill the frame. The shot is crowded with people on the move and Cop 223 pushes against the people just to make his way through the throng. He is escorting a criminal through the streets but this is only established through fragmentary cuts to handcuffed hands, and a paper bag that has been placed over the criminal's head. The same musical score and street noise have continued right across the pillow shots and the shots of the Cop pushing his way through the street, so that aurally, the fragmentary images and loosely connected planes of action are brought together.

The sequence then sets up a further foreshadow: as Cop 223 makes his way through the street he takes interest in a female mannequin being hoisted through the crowd on someone's shoulder. He turns to look at the mannequin at the exact moment she appears to 'metamorphose' into the Blonde Woman. This 'simulated' first contact encounter provides the motor for the criminal to make his escape, and sets in play the idea of desire for the dangerous Blonde Woman being a form of danger itself.

In the chase sequence that follows, stretch-printing is used for the first time: Cop 223 moves across the screen in slow-motion while the crowds around him rush by in fast time. The effects of this are super sensuous and yet highly melancholic. The traces of neon colours and smudged faces create the sense that one is watching a moving canvass. The cuts are rapid, and across the whole scene they often break the axis of action so that people move in contradictory ways, and space itself seems unstable and unreliable. Cop 223 is caught up in this bewildering hyper-reality, and is being marked out as someone out of time, alone and lonely in this city with a different pulse and tempo, and where space itself turns on him. He is, in effect, a 'mirror' of the Blonde Woman, whose doppelganger has got him into this mess in the first place.

Seconds later, as fate/chance would have it, he 'brushes' into the 'real' Blonde Woman, framed in front of a fruit and veg market stall, although the viewer has very little time to make

'Freeze!'

A moving canvas

0.01cm away from love

the connection. The encounter initially lasts for less than a second but at the exact moment they do 'meet' the film then makes another abrupt and discontinuous (metaphoric) cut. The audience is suddenly placed in an anonymous room, rather like a bank, with a clock foregrounded in the front of the shot. At almost the exact second we cut to the clock, which is the exact second that they meet, the time changes from (Friday 28 April) 8.59 to 9.00. In this 'remembered' encounter time is recorded with finite detail and reverie – for Cop 223 this moment will last forever.

But the centrality of deadlines, of counting down, of time

running out is also being established and in a direct sense the countdown has now literally begun in the film. The starting pistol has gone off, and the race to fall in love, to close down or shut off time so that one does fall in love, has begun. But in truth, Cop 223 also wants to efface his own voice-over, to make time go backwards, so that the despair he finds himself in, in the aching present, never actually happens. He doesn't really want the memory of this moment to last forever, but the moment to be changed and for that 'utopian' moment to become real and to last forever. In his memory, played out in the voice-over monologue, when the clock hits 9.00, he wants them to fall in love at that precise moment and not later. Of course, this cannot happen: the clock, the clouds move on regardless. His memory will have to do.

But the memory is actually only one of distant (albeit) sensuous intimacy. As the clock turns to 9.00, the scene cuts back to the Cop and the Blonde Woman 'nearly' touching. In what becomes a poetic dance, she turns full circle on her heels, and they share a fleeting glimpse (of each other) as he rushes past. However, they are connected in a kinetic sense. She shares the slow-motion timeframe that has carried him through the rest of the sequence, so that even in this short exchange, they exist in the same space, at the same time, whereas in contrast, the rest of the world is out of kilter with them. Just for the briefest of moments, then, they are the only two people in the world that matter.

Of course, the whole sequence works in relation to the other main themes of the film. The 'countdown' scenario speaks to the pending hand-over of Hong Kong to the Chinese in 1997. The search for love, for a home, is one borne out of a desperate sense of loneliness in a city that has no centre, no linear lines of movement and no familial networks. The references to Hollywood cinema foreground the film's (critical)

obsession with American culture, and popular culture more generally. The scene ends with Cop 223 uttering, in voice-over, the immortal lines, 'At our closest point, we were just .01cm apart. 55 hours later, I was in love with this woman.' Distance, measurement, the mechanics of time, they work their influence across the film, like a spectre or ghost, never being fully pinned down, but always totally in control of their movement and circularity. Fade to black.

Conclusion

0.01cm Away From Love

The potential for intimacy

It seems that in *Chungking Express* anyone is only ever 0.01cm away from love, from romance, from truly belonging. At all times, all the characters seem desperately close to having their fantasies, desires and utopian dreams fulfilled. But even this tiny gap between Cop 223 and the Blonde Woman, and Cop 663 and Faye, produces disappointment, despair and a deep yearning/need for the gap to be closed. And yet, paradoxically, when the opportunities emerge for real fleshy connection between the characters, they run away from one another. Cop 223 watches TV, eats Chef salads while the woman he has fallen in love with sleeps. It doesn't seem to cross his mind to get in bed with her, to caress her soft skin, to close the gap. Faye takes flight when confronted by Cop 663 and the now tangible possibility that they will be intimate with one another. She stands him up at the California bar, and makes her way to the 'real' California, in effect increasing the gap between them.

The core motif that one is only 0.01cm away from love is constructed in a number of ways in the film. Telecommunications provide the gap to converse, to leave messages, to record one's desires, without being in the exact same, close proximity space as the other person. Chance encounters that don't quite work out in terms of the precise collision between time and space structure the love affairs in the film. At the beginning of the film, Cop 223 manages to avoid literally falling into/onto the Blonde Woman, asserting the importance of the gap between them. If he had fallen into her arms the sexual outcome between them might have been very different. Faye is seen constantly cleaning, tidying and rearranging Cop 663's apartment, and yet until the very end of the film, never bumps into him (in his own space!). Goods and food establish or maintain the gap between people. The jilted Cop 223 devours his girlfriend's favourite food because he can no longer have her; the Blonde Woman establishes distance with the drug boss through her commodity disguise (he never gets really close to the real woman, behind the mask); and Cop 663 gets close to Faye through buying the Midnight Express where she used to work.

However, the sense that one is always in close proximity to love and romance can be seen to be a highly positive thing, as if the world is constantly charged by, or at least is on stand-by for the possibility of the intimate encounter. To be always potentially a fraction of a measurement away from someone who you could love forever, is simply electric. Hong Kong provides the potential for this sensuous type of intimacy because of its population density, and diversity in goods, experiences and spaces.

Chungking Express is a mixed-up film much in the way that the characters are themselves mixed-up (over love, their own identities, desires and needs). In one sense it is clearly influenced by European Art Cinema, and in particular the work of Jean-Luc Godard. In another, it is clearly influenced by (Hollywood) genres, MTV style music videos, and the signs and codes of popular culture more generally. *Chungking Express* seems to be critical of the influence of goods, brands, and the media on everyday Hong Kong life; and yet, at the same time, it seems to celebrate the aura of the commodity and the consumption space. *Chungking Express* pays homage to American culture and yet also shows American culture to be hackneyed and empty of any deep, interior meaning (it is ultimately disposable). *Chungking Express* seems to be nostalgic for a romantic Hong Kong past of cultural diversity, and fearful of a future under Chinese rule. *Chungking Express* is a schizophrenic film, full of schizophrenic characters, and diverse and contradictory reference points. But this is what makes the film so fascinating, so thought provoking, so beautifully memorable. One is only ever 0.01cm away from falling in love with this film.

Recommended Bibliography and Filmography

Bibliography

Bordwell, David (2000) **Planet Hong Kong: Popular Cinema and the Art of Entertainment**, London: Harvard University Press.

Bordwell, David (2002) 'The Art Cinema as a Mode of Film Practice', in Fowler, Catherine (ed.) **The European Cinema Reader**, London: Routledge.

Brooker, Peter and Brooker, Will (eds) (1997) **Postmodern AfterImages**, London: Arnold.

Chow, Rey (1999) 'Nostalgia of the New Wave: Structure in Wong Kar-wai's *Happy Together*', in **Camera Obscura**, September, Volume 14, Issue 42, pages 31–50.

Cook, Pam and Bernink, Mieke (eds) (1999) **The Cinema Book 2nd edition**, London: BFI.

Deleuze, Gilles, 'On the Movement-Image', trans. Martin Joughin, **Negotiations: 1972–1990**, New York: Columbia University Press, 1985

Deleuze, Gilles, **Cinema 1: The Movement-Image**, trans. Hugh Tomlinson and Barbara Habberjam, Minneapolis: University of Minnesota Press, 1986; and **Cinema 2: The Time-Image**, trans. Hugh Tomlinson and Robert Galeta, London: Athlone Press, 1989

Gan, Wendy (2003) '0.01cm: Affectivity and Urban Space in *Chungking Express*', in **Scope: An Online Journal of Film Studies**, Nottingham: University of Nottingham.

Gross, Larry (1996) 'Nonchalant Grace', in **Sight and Sound**, September, Volume 6, Issues 9, pages 9–10.

Kwai-Cheung Lo (2001) 'Transnationalization of the Local in Hong Kong Cinema', in Yau, Esther C.M. (ed.) **At Full Speed: Hong Kong Cinema in a Borderless World**, Minnesota: University of Minnesota Press.

Lalanne, Jean-Marc, Martinez, David, Abbas, Ackbar and Ngai, Jimmy (eds) (1997) **Wong Kar-wai**, Paris: Dis Voir.

Marchetti, Gina (2000) 'Buying American, Consuming Hong Kong: Cultural Commerce, Fantasies of Identity, and the Cinema', in Desser, David and Fu, Poshek (eds) **The Cinema of Hong Kong**, Cambridge: Cambridge University Press.

Martinez, David (1997) 'Chasing the Metaphysical Express', in Lalanne, Jean-Marc et al (eds) (1997) **Wong Kar-Wai**, Paris: Dis Voir.

Mazierska, Ewa and Rascaroli, Laura, (2000) 'Trapped in the Present: Time in the Films of Wong Kar-wai', in **Film Criticism**, Winter, Volume 25, Issue 2, pages 2–20.

Mcluhan, Marshal (1989) **The Global Village**, Oxford: Oxford University Press.

Neale, Steve (2002) 'Art Cinema as Institution', in Fowler, Catherine (ed.) **The European Cinema Reader**, London: Routledge.

Poster, Mark (1988) **Jean Baudrillard**, London: Polity.

Siegel, Marc (2001) 'The Intimate Spaces of Wong Kar-wai', in Ester C.M. Yau (ed.) **At Full Speed: Hong Kong Cinema in a Borderless World**, Minnesota: University of Minnesota Press.

Stokes, Lisa and Hoover, Michael (1999) **City on Fire: Hong Kong Cinema**, London: Verso.

Tambling, Jeremy (2003) **Wong Kar-wai's** *Happy Together*, Hong Kong: Hong Kong University Press.

Thompson, John B. (1995) **The Media and Modernity**, London: Polity Press.

Tong, Janice (2003) '*Chungking Express*: Time and its Displacements', in Berry, Chris (ed.) **Chinese Films in Focus: 25 New Takes**, London: BFI.

Yau, Easther (ed.) (2001) **At Full Speed: Hong Kong Cinema in a Borderless World**, Minneapolis, Minnesota: University of Minnesota Press.

Filmography

Double Indemnity (Wilder, 1944)

A bout de Souffle (Godard, 1960)

Dangerous Encounter of the First Kind (Hark, 1980)

Handsworth Songs (Akomprah, 1986)

Final Victory (Tam, 1987)

Funny Games (Haneke, 1997)

Wong Kar-wai Filmography

As Tears Go By (1988)

Days of Being Wild (1991)

Ashes of Time (1994)

Fallen Angels (1995)

Happy Together (1997)

In the Mood for Love (2000)

2046 (2004)

My Blueberry Nights (2007)

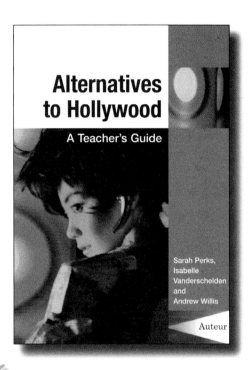

"The ideal introduction to three non-Anglo/
American cinemas - French, Indian and East
Asian, including a case-study of the Hong Kong
New Wave and director Wong Kar-wai."

Studying Blade Runner
Sean Redmond

Also Available from Auteur

Studying City of God
Stephanie Muir

"This is one of the best study guides I have seen... you would be foolish indeed to ignore this guide."

In the Picture

Studying The Matrix
Anna Dawson

Anna Dawson feels that *The Matrix* is far more substantial than it first looks, and her enthusiasm for the film... is not only valuable, but ultimately infectious.

Times Educational Supplement

NOTES

NOTES

NOTES

NOTES

NOTES

NOTES

NOTES

NOTES